A GUIDE TO

SMALL WATER
TROUT FISHING

IN THE SOUTH

D1386338

A GUIDE TO

SMALL WATER TROUT FISHING

IN THE SOUTH

GRAEME PULLEN

Ashford Press Publishing
Southampton
1989

Published by Ashford Press Publishing
1 Church Road
Shedfield
Hampshire
SO3 2HW

The author would like to thank all the fishery owners who assisted him with factual information for this book.

British Library Cataloguing in Publication Data

Pullen, Graeme
 A guide to small water trout fishing
 in the South.
 1.   Southern England. Angling Water.
 Trout fisheries.
 I.   Title
 799.1′755

ISBN 1-85253-117-7

Typeset by Acorn Bookwork, Salisbury, Wiltshire
Printed by Hartnolls Limited, Bodmin, Cornwall, England

Cover photograph: the author netting a good rainbow from the middle beat of the river at Rockbourne Fishery.

*To Charlotte Louise, a beautiful daughter,
and hopefully a good fisherwoman!*

SELECTED TROUT FISHERIES
IN THE SOUTH OF ENGLAND

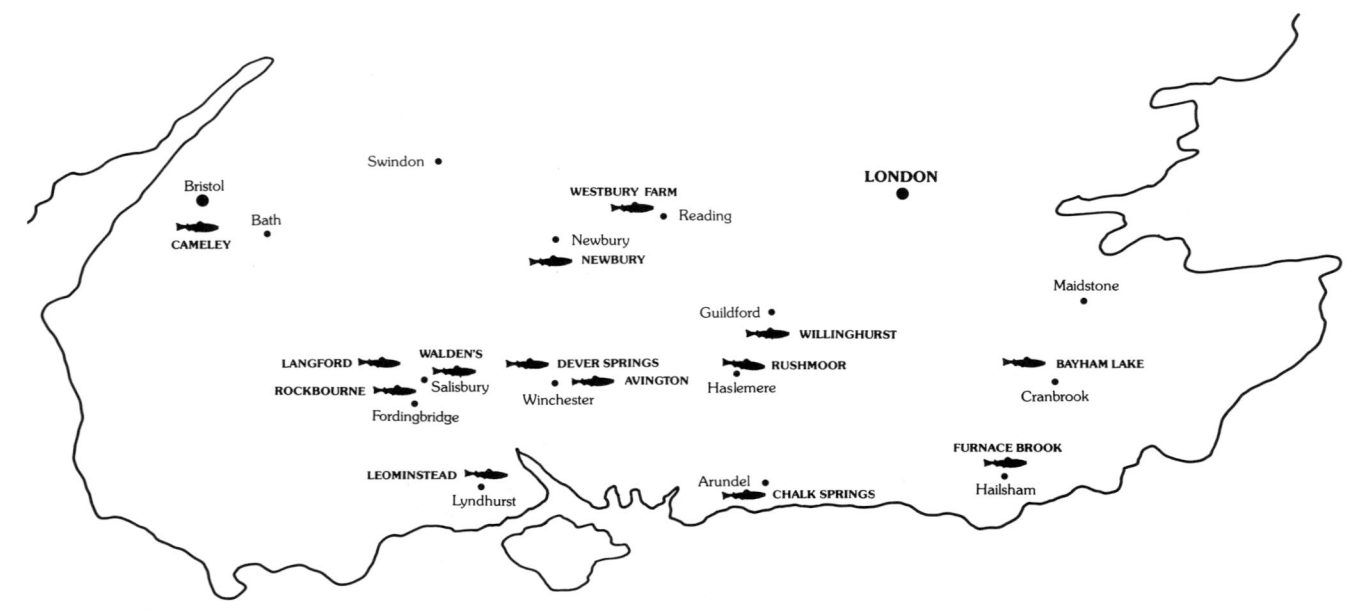

Contents

List of Photographs

List of Maps

INTRODUCTION

I set myself the task of writing this guide mainly because of the huge void that exists in the book market. As a photojournalist I am always looking for new material, and having recently become disillusioned with magazines, I turned to the world of books. Why not, I concluded, give the fly fisherman a guide he could pick up at any time in order to choose a venue of which he may have had no previous experience? Lord knows it's infuriating to fish new waters for an entire day with a black fly, only to learn on your return to the lodge that everything always comes out on a white fly! I make no attempt at beguiling the reader with the complexities of higher entomology. I feel that, like me, you will want a fish or two on your line and in a reasonably short time. You may also be relieved to learn that I have no personal vested interest in any fishery. The venues I have included are all waters I have visited myself, so you will get in each case an unbiased appraisal from an ordinary trout angler like yourself.

I cannot throw a steeple cast through a six-inch gap, change direction mid-cast, then roll-cast backwards to a trout 50 yards away under a hawthorn bush! My trout have come the hard way, through many water hours and constant fly changes. I have left as many flies up the trees as the next man, and have no shame in fishing for an hour before discovering I have eight wind knots in the leader! What I try to apply to my own fishing is not so much refined technique, as a honed instinct. Just where would you be if *you* were the trout? Where are the weedbeds? the insects? the fry? Which bank does the prevailing wind blow into? A lot of the time the location of the trout is of more importance than the choice of fly. Find a feeding fish and you should obtain a response in just three fly changes.

The small water trout fisheries are here to stay and provide thousands of fishermen with the chance to catch a good-sized rainbow or brown in conditions that are often sheltered, with clear water, and where there is a stocking density that at least assures you of as much success as the next man. I am not a writer who fishes only on press days, when the stocking density can be so ridiculously high that the trout border on the suicidal. I did once hammer 34 trout on such a press day, and while it may be classed as entertainment, I attach no significance at all to the catch. A press day usually provides a chance to test a new rod, reel, leader, fly, or technique on a fish. I have similar feelings about the super-big trout, the jumbos of 15 lb and above. Not a case of sour grapes I assure you, but I have visited many of the top fisheries that produce the monsters, and have yet to see one over that weight, either in the water or on the bank. And I can promise you I know how to spot fish, especially when they come two and a half feet long!

Again, press days can also be times when big fish are stocked. The problem the fishery owners have are twofold. First, a 15 lb rainbow trout will have cost a small fortune to feed on to that size, and represents a financial outlay appreciated by very few anglers. This fish will have been fed for years exclusively on a high-protein diet of pellet-based food. Then it is dropped into a lake, and I don't care what anyone tells me: there is not a water in Britain that can sustain a 15 lb rainbow on insect life alone. Therefore, the fishery owner needs that fish to be caught as soon as possible, before it starts to 'go back', or lose weight. Moreover, he will want to see some publicity from the capture of such a fish, which he is not so likely to get if an 'ordinary' angler catches it. Therefore he needs plenty of people on the day the big fish are stocked, several of whom must be useful with a 35 mm camera.

I think the late Dick Walker was correct when he said that a record fish is merely an indication of how big a particular species grows, and you have to admire him for not claiming the British record with that 18 lb fish of his. Therefore on the subject of jumbo trout I leave you to draw your own conclusions. You will not find this book littered with pictures of jumbos all caught by the same person. I fish when the average angler fishes. I hear his moans, his groans, his opinions, and his delights, so I am in an excellent position to write as balanced an account of each water as you are ever likely to get. Many fishery owners will appreciate this, as it is you, the travelling angler, that they most wish to visit their waters.

You may follow my advice, enjoy a blinding treble limit of trout, and write something nice in the log book. Or you may fail, and write something less tasteful. But I think you will agree, after putting this book to the test, that I have endeavoured to give you the best my pen and camera can produce. After all, like yourself, I am simply a trout angler interested in a good day's fishing!

HOW DO TROUT GET THERE?

Almost every angler has some idea of how trout grow, and there are many reliable books on the intricacies of the subject. Modern methods of research into the various diseases and their causes and treatment made the art of trout farming a more secure occupation. It may interest a few of the newcomers to learn about its basics, and in this way they will appreciate fully that the trout they catch are hand-fed, and not wild.

There has always raged a controversy over the merits of wild as opposed to artificially reared trout. As the pressure on flyfishing has increased, so the demand for value-for-money wild trout fisheries has become impractical. A hundred years ago trout fishing was undertaken mainly in flowing water, and the primary species was the brown trout. Then along came the fast-growing rainbow with its acrobatics on being hooked, its culinary virtues, and its freedom in taking the fisherman's fly. In addition, the rainbow was a faster grower than the brown, and therefore soon took over. While a truly wild fish is one that has been laid as an egg by another wild fish, and grows to a good size under normal conditions, the rainbow presents a complete contrast. Rarely do rainbow trout breed in the wild, and what is now thought of as a 'wild' fish is one introduced into a large reservoir as a fingerling, and which, fending for itself, grows to a respectable size.

While the small stillwater fisheries stock with fish bigger on average than those in reservoirs, a fish from the latter is a whole different ball game when hooked. A reservoir rainbow leaps more, has more stamina, has no damaged fins, and displays a full silver body that defies description. As a fingerling it will still have been reared artificially, but it is 'free range', as opposed to 'battery'. All the small stillwater farms do is to feed the fish longer. To get a proper insight into this, I interviewed the manager of Avington Fisheries, Roy Ward.

Few would dispute the fast growth rate of the Avington rainbow, and they have taken the British record for a variety of trout species over the years. First you need pure, clean spring water. Although the stock ponds at Avington are fed by the river Itchen, the egg and fry hatchery is fed only by pure bore-hole water, so that it is as clean as possible. As a basis for a good egg, you need a good stock to breed from. Roy looks after his brood fish to ensure that when he strips the eggs, only the best are produced. He has refined a fast-growing strain of trout, so why should he let it deteriorate? Roy strips the fish throughout November, and although some text books state that 700 eggs come from each pound of body weight, he thinks that it may go as high as 2000 for an 8 lb rainbow. He runs a batch of brood fish in

Avington's fishery manager Roy Ward runs his bore-hole water straight through these large glass jars. Inside are thousands of trout eggs, the pure, highly oxygenated water maximizing the hatch rate of eggs. The water runs through the eggs, then spills over the edge of the jars.

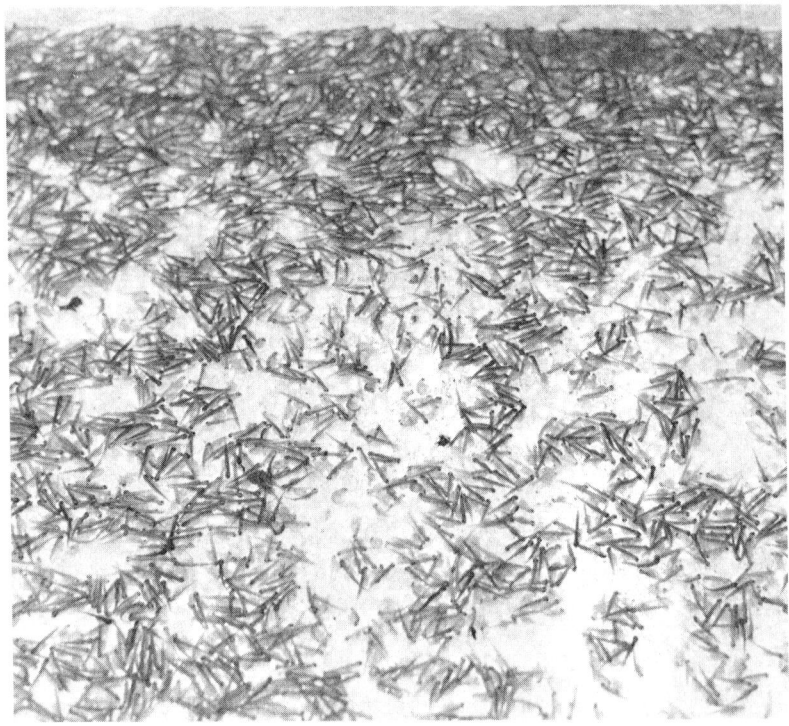

Once hatched, the fry are moved to darkened shallow troughs, with highly oxygenated water running through to ensure healthy fish. At this stage they are fed with a powdered food with a high protein content.

the 7–10 lb range. You can usually reckon on stripping milt from one male and mixing it with the eggs of three females, but Roy sometimes uses a one-to-one mixture.

After fertilization, the eggs are placed in incubator jars, each holding about five gallons of water, and mounted some 2 ft from the floor. This method allows Roy to use the minimum area for the maximum eggs, whereas some trout farms use up a lot of floor space by placing them in trays. The water from the bore hole is run through a 'header' tank by gravity feed, to oxygenate the water as much as possible before it runs through the incubator jars. Roy can hold 100,000 eggs in each jar, the water pressure gently vibrating the eggs for a slight movement. Mortality during this critical egg stage is understandably high, but from the egg stage to saleable fish Roy reckons he has a 60 per cent success rate.

The eggs hatch in 26 days and are then placed in concrete raceways, where natural spring water is run through the shallow troughs. The hatching eggs are suspended in fine metal trays, which allow the hatching fry to drop through, leaving the dead eggs and underdeveloped fry in the tray for easy removal. They stay in these concrete raceways for three to four weeks, feeding only on the remains of their eggs sacks. After this stage they start to take the first of the high-protein feed, which comes first as a fine powder and is later given as graded grains of feed. (Avington gets through a staggering 15 tons of high-protein trout feed each season.) The Fry are kept in the raceways until they weigh approximately one hundred fish to the pound, at which time it is safe enough to take them out into the river water, the bore-hole water being almost free of diseases and bacteria. There are many different diseases, but as the fry continue to grow, they develop their own system of natural defence.

The following November, exactly one year after the egg was mixed with the milt, the fish will be about 9 in in length, but fish farms supplying the table trade will push their fish even larger by intensive feeding. For the stocking of another water most fisheries now require a 2 lb fish, which would be around two years old. After three years of feeding, Roy has a 7–10 lb fish, while a four year old may be 9–15 lb, and a five year old 20 lb. Roy explained that, just like humans and animals, some fish turn out to be faster growers than others. He thinks they could go on just over five years, while others think rainbows could live longer than eight years. As a guide, wild browns in a natural feeding environment may grow to even ten or twelve years old.

As well as pushing around 12,000 2 lb–plus rainbows through his farming facility, Roy has seen all the hybrids: the tiger trout, which was a brook brown cross; the cheetah, which is a brook rainbow cross; and the brookie itself, which is a species in its own right, and related to the char. He can deliver his stock anywhere by pumping a water tank full of highly oxygenated water, using commercial oxygen bottles. It is even possible to transport fish internationally by aircraft.

In Canada and the United States trout are 'seeded' into an inaccessible water by dropping them from a low-flying aircraft as it skims the surface.

There you have a glimpse of how a fish farm produces the trout you catch from a small stillwater. Fish farms supply both the food trade and the requirements of fishermen. Whether you agree with intensive feeding or not, the small waters are here to fill a void, and if there were no such farms, then you would have few trout to catch.

When they have reached several inches, the fry are taken from the hatchery troughs and placed outside in the open stews. Roy Ward feeds the stock ponds several times a day, their surface boiling as thousands of fish race to grab the pellets. From here they are graded to separate the fast growers from standard stock. The next item of food they see should be the angler's fly, when they have been stocked into the lakes.

CHOOSING TACKLE

The selection and use of fly fishing tackle can always be left to the individual. Assuming you have a basic grasp of what a fly rod, reel, and line look like, and understand the principles that make them work, you should address your attention to the actual fishing. Too many people seem to get caught up with 'posing' with all the 'right' tackle, partly because the sport of trout fishing is traditionally fashionable. As for the flies themselves, fishermen all over the world are constantly on the prowl for the magic pattern that will have trout falling over themselves to grab it. By contrast, I was never one to follow fashions; nor did I swagger round the fisheries with all the lastest super equipment. My concern has always been to sink a hook into a trout's jaw, and to that end I have been fairly successful.

Once you have tried other aspects of the sport, it is easy to drop into flyfishing. I have no hesitation in stating that one of the most incredibly stupid and gullible fish is the trout. It is so easy to catch by normal methods that it had to be protected by restricting tactics to casting a fly. If you care to run a freelined lobworm down the River Itchen or put a Mepps spinner in one of the River Test pools you would see how gullible trout can be. You would also be hung, drawn, and quartered, so I mention this purely tongue in cheek.

Flycasting is in itself a pleasurable way of casting, but what about the properties of a fly rod for applying pressure to a fish? Or that tiny reel, invariably without a drag system save for the clicker mechanism? I think the time has come for manufacturers to launch into some new centre drag fly reels, or rods with an extendable butt to allow the rod blank to be flexed along the forearm. But then these are my ideas, and after you have spent a few years 'under the rod' yourself, you too may feel there is room for a change. The basic fly rod for any of the stillwaters described in this book should be of carbon fibre, or a carbon/fibreglass mix, and about 9ft long. There is little need for ultra-long casts, and to that end the line weight should be a little over that of the rod's capabilities. An overrated line-to-rod ratio will ensure you fire out the casts better, and should that line be of the weight-forward variety, then your mistakes will be ironed out by the carrying capacity of the line.

You need just three types of line. I have been using Airflo lines for a while now and they seem to have the edge in quality. For dry fly and nymph fishing you will need a floating line. There are intermediates and slow sinks but if you are a complete newcomer to flyfishing, the last thing you want is to be baffled by the range of different line weights available. To the floating line you attach your nylon leader, which should be around 9 ft long, but perhaps as long as 12 ft on hot, still summer days. This can be degreased with a sinking paste which allows you to retrieve a nymph or small lure just beneath the surface. Or you can grease it with a mucilin leader floatant which ensures your dry fly will stay on top of the surface film. So with the one floating line you have two options to try.

I would then advise going to a medium-sink line, which for most of the depths you are likely to encounter in the fisheries listed, is quite sufficient. You can fish a medium-sink as deep as you want simply by waiting longer for the line to drop through the depths. My advice is to try a retrieve after, say, ten seconds, then twenty, then thirty, trying to remember the number when you hit a fish. This is called the countdown technique and is ideal for a thorough search of the depths.

If you are fishing a deep pool or hole, knowing full well that the fish are down deep, then use a fast-sink line. This heavier line is better suited to late-autumn and winter fishing, when the water temperatures will have pushed the trout deeper and made them more lethargic. Your best bet with a fast-sink line is to grease the leader, and use a buoyant pattern of fly such as a muddler. This stops the hook picking up leaves, twigs, and other rubbish deposited on the lake bed during the gales of late autumn, and fishes the fly well inside the trout's 'kill' zone. This technique of using a greased leader and a sunk line allows you to fish very slowly with your retrieve, which is very useful since the trout takes will be more gentle in colder weather.

You can choose any fly reel, as in my opinion they are all merely line-storage devices. Until someone comes up with a geared, centre-drag fly reel my view will remain unchanged. You need two fly boxes. A wallet with a styrofoam insert is ideal for nymphs and lures. With dry flies you need to ensure that they are loose and that the hackles are not crushed. Treat yourself to one of those multi-partitioned fly boxes with hinged lids. Watch out for windy weather when you open it, as a gust of wind can deposit all your best dry flies over half the country-side, where they will blend in superbly! You need a good landing net, preferably a 20-inch model with a telescopic or extending handle. You need a priest to whack the trout over the head. Don't waste good money on a shop-bought priest – a small piece of copper tube with some lead packed in one end does the same job.

Flyfishing jackets are great on summer days, when you can wander around with the bare minimum of gear. But how many fine days do we get? By all means get one, but choose a heavier coat like a Barbour to cope with all weather conditions. You'll need a good hat with a broad peak to shut down the sunlight. I use a professional guide's hat with sunflaps for the ears and neck. You can buy them in the USA, and quite why nobody has started importing them into the UK yet is beyond me. You need a pair of good polarizing glasses – not just to cut down the glare, but to cut down the risk of planting your fly in your eyeball. I saw a photo once of an angler with a fly lodged about $\frac{1}{8}$ in in his eye, right past the barb, and a whisker from his pupil! I never forgot that picture and fish in glasses even in the rain! The best tint to get is brown, though the grey glasses are good. You will also, I hope, require a wicker bag to carry your fish around. If it is high summer, gut them at the fishing hut as soon as possible and place them in a cool box, as they can go off in a few hours of freak summer sunshine. The ASW Coolfishbag is custom-made for keeping fish chilled, and can also be used for the angler's own food.

Finally, start to take an interest in fly tying as early as you can. It serves to expand your knowledge of exactly what a fly does under water, enables you to make up your patterns and of course you save an enormous amount of money on shop flies. Buy a few to copy, then make your own flies. Good hunting!

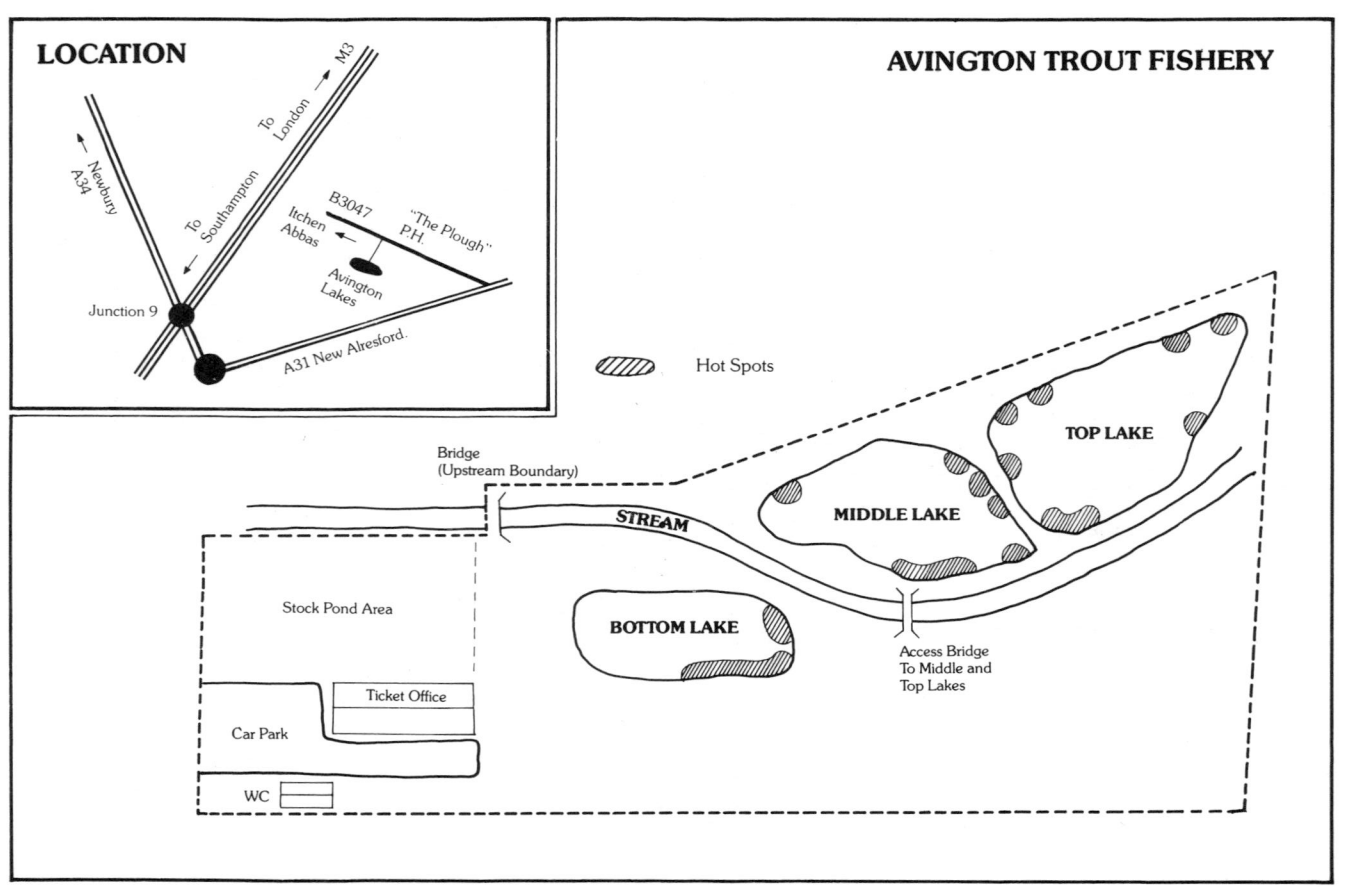

LOCATION

To London
M3

To Southampton

Newbury
A34

B3047

"The Plough" P.H.

Itchen Abbas

Avington Lakes

Junction 9

A31 New Alresford.

AVINGTON TROUT FISHERY

Hot Spots

TOP LAKE

MIDDLE LAKE

Bridge
(Upstream Boundary)

STREAM

Access Bridge
To Middle and
Top Lakes

Stock Pond Area

BOTTOM LAKE

Ticket Office

Car Park

WC

AVINGTON

If there is a fishery of which all trout anglers must have heard, then it is Avington. Certainly no other water has retained such a firm grip on the British record for rainbow trout. This fishery, more than any other, is responsible for creating first-class trout fishing in stillwater that all anglers can afford. The main reason for its incredible popularity is that you never really know when a new record is about to be introduced. The largest brown trout to come out on a fly came from this fishery . . . at over 13 lb. It has also held all the other trout records at one time or other – for rainbow, brook, tiger and cheetah – but the next few years will see only rainbows stocked. However, the largest that Roy Ward has swimming around in his stock pond is 27 lb!

Personally, I feel that a true British record for any trout must be based on a fish that has grown on from a small stockfish. Yet even though Avington uses the same production methods as most other fish farms, they still produce the biggest number of double-figure trout every season. While you may not agree with stocking policies which include the jumbo trout, they are here to stay, and have proven beyond doubt that anglers will always want the chance of holding the record, whether it is with a fed-on stockfish or a wild fish.

Now I have to point out something that is clear to me as a businessman, but still causes a few gripes from the average fisherman. To grow a rainbow on into double figures and beyond requires a lot of intensive feeding with a high-protein food, usually in pellet form. This food is a concentrate and is expensive. The more years a trout spends in the stock pond, the more it costs the fishery owner. There is simply no way that any trout fishery can make a profit if every angler catches a limit of 3 lb rainbows, let alone double-figure fish. A fishery is in business, so before you start moaning that you haven't caught four 10 lb trout, remember that fact. It just cannot

Surely the most famous of all the small trout venues, Avington, in Hampshire, first started the ball rolling with double-figure rainbows. It remains capable of producing another British record. Here Adrian Hutchins from Guildford reaches out to net a good fish in the first lake.

afford for all the anglers to catch a limit of big fish, and most of the profits are courtesy of the fisherman who blanks. The more trout you catch, the more you eat away at the profit margin.

Looking at most of the fisheries' reports as I do, I would say they all aim for an average catch of about 2.5 fish per angler. Anything above that reduces their profit; anything below and the anglers stop coming because they feel the water is understocked. To attain this 'average' most waters will overstock on the fish-per-acre-of-water density to allow for pricked fish, fish broken off, and the odd one that dies. They also have to allow for the unfortunate fact of anglers stealing fish by taking more than their limit. You can perhaps now see that there is more to running a fishery as a business enterprise than just tipping a few trout in a lake. Avington hosts a fair few fish over 5 lb on almost every day of fishing, and certainly the chance of taking a double-figure trout is there, but don't forget that there will also be a lot around the 2–3 lb mark, which are still fine fish to catch.

The fishery came into being about sixteen years ago when the $13\frac{1}{4}$ acres of property was all one lake. All once part of a large estate, the land was then sectioned up and sold off. The fishery lies in one of the last unpolluted areas in England, the Itchen valley, and the water quality is excellent. The chalk hills act as filters, and the underground aquifers supply a constant flow of water through summer and winter. Many who have fished there will not realize that the sidestream of the Itchen that feeds both stock ponds and lakes is manmade. The late Sam Holland actually dug the stream to take the water out of the lake in order that he could landscape it and construct three lakes, the stock ponds, and build the bungalow as a residence. One of the more pleasant pastimes is to spend a couple of hours trying to catch a fish out of the stream, which I personally find more rewarding than tackling the lakes.

The Itchen is mainly syndicated as a trout stream, and rarely comes under any sort of fishing pressure. It starts as a serious trout stream when the Arle and Tichbourne Brook join together. Then it becomes possibly the most famous trout river in British flyfishing history. They run down into Southampton water, with access to any of the fishing extremely difficult. The result of this pure chalkstream water is that the lakes at Avington can go gin-clear, making sighting an individual fish a very stimulating method. I would go so far as to say that if you want a big trout, then visual location is an absolute necessity.

There are certain holding areas in each of the three lakes, and not only the deeper areas, but the number of trout stocked was discovered only when I visited the water last winter. Manager Roy Ward was in the process of dredging the centre lake of silt and altering the layout of the bank. Even he was amazed to find over a hundred trout in the one deep end of the centre lake, when everyone thought it had been completely netted! It goes to show that a lot of rainbows skulk off into a dark hole or under the weed and so elude the angler's attempts to lure them out!

APPROACH AND TACKLE

The half a mile or so of the Itchen tributary, from the bridge below the stock ponds to the bridge at the bottom end of the fishery, is narrow and is best fished with a light rod, a No. 5 line, and weighted nymphs. The trout get used to seeing anglers, so you need a very careful approach. I suggest locating a trout, then sitting and waiting at least five minutes before you even make a cast. Any weighted nymph should get a response, and remember that there are a few decent fish in here from time to time. The largest fish I ever took on a dry fly weighed 4 lb 1 oz and came just a few yards down from where the stream starts. It may help you to walk the stream first, taking a mental note of where you spook the fish from, and then return to that area a few hours after fishing the lakes.

To fish the first lake, I suggest that, when the initial five-seconds-past-starting-time rush gets off, you walk along the left-hand side. Most anglers take off down the right-hand side, but the sunlight will be in your eyes if you do likewise. The left bank is slightly higher towards the end and, with the light behind you, sighting a fish is easier. Casting may be tricky but that is half the fun! The average depth of the first lake is about 6 ft, deepening to 9 ft at the bottom end. It is very sheltered, so don't be suprised if you get a rise of trout in the afternoon. It won't be the bigger fish, as they rarely rise, but mostly fish in the 2–2½ lb bracket, which can present interesting prospects.

While you may be tempted to walk past the first few 3 lb 'stockies', take my advice and catch one, maybe two, of them. You don't know for sure that the better fishing is in the middle and lower lakes, and with a couple of early fish under your belt, you can afford to walk the lakes spotting for larger quarry. Nearly all the fish that are easy takers will come out in the first twenty minutes, and I have even finished my day's fishing at 9.16 AM! This is not due to anything clever – just an unusually high stocking density. It is great for 16 minutes, but leaves you with nothing to do for the rest of the day. The best places in the first lake are at each end, with the better fishing being at the far end.

The middle lake is the largest of the eight acres of water, around

3 ft deep at the inflow end, where it is silted up, and averaging 9 ft. Of three good places to try as soon as you get there, the first is the inlet. Stay only for a few pulls through, and then move to the right-hand bank. About midway along here the backcasting area is clear and you can get a good cast out. Work the area thoroughly, moving up or down for 20 yards until you find the fish. Invariably, though, they will find you! Then the main hotspot is at the bottom end of this lake, where the trout will circle around in the deeper water. You may not spot them in the deeper water, but it is here that Roy netted the final inches of water when he dropped the level for dredging.

The third, or lower, lake is where many of the big trout now come

The clarity of the water at Avington calls for careful stalking along the margins if you are to have the best chance of finding the bigger trout. Usually the first angler to present his fly correctly to a big fish will find himself attached to a bundle of fun! This angler stalks a fish on the first lake.

out. Immediately where it joins the middle lake is the deepest part of the entire fishery. The 'hole', as it is known, drops away to 14 ft, so that it is not often that you see the bigger fish cruising the bottom. The middle section of this lower lake is usually devoid of any but the odd fish or two. However, the extreme bottom end by the overhanging trees, where it empties out, is an excellent area for big trout, so take a careful look through this pool.

As for the stream itself, I would say that the upstream one-third is more productive than the lower two-thirds. This advice should optimize your time spent at the water, but a word of caution is necessary about the weed. In high summer all lakes warm up and display a profusion of weed. In this respect Avington is no different and has growths of Canadian Pondweed, as well as some algal blooms. These algal growths may be a pest at first but on a weedy day they can actually pinpoint the fish for you. The weed will die off and then float to the surface, drifting wherever the breeze takes it. Forming itself into large mats, it both provides the trout with an area of shade and gives them a sense of security since they cannot see the angler. On a breezy day it will mat up solidly and drift hard against a corner of bank.

Working a heavy nymph along the edge of this weed mat has given many anglers a big trout, and some even develop their own way of getting to fish. All they do is poke a hole in the weed and then lower a heavily weighted nymph through, making it rise and fall with the rod top. They call it 'jiggling', and it certainly hooks fish when they won't come out to the edge of the weedbed. The problem is not in hooking fish, but getting them out. Use an 8 lb leader and hold the fish as hard as you dare. Fly line has no stretch except in the leader tippet, which at close range takes some pretty hard punishment! Not my idea of flyfishing, but a useful method when everything else fails.

SEASONAL TACTICS

Spring

Being a chalk stream, the water feeding the lakes should have a fairly consistent temperature, which means that the trout should be in

The author displays a bumper rainbow trout from one of Avington's lakes. Make sure you have a leader of at least 6 lb breaking strain, and use polarizing sunglasses to enable you to spot the fish individually. This fish fell to a 'Bumblenymph', a pattern designed by the author. Heavily weighted nymphs probably account for more big trout at this venue than any other method.

feeding mood and searching through the middle-to-lower levels. Weed growth will be minimal, so you should use a medium sinking line, No. 7 or 8, a rod to match, and a leader tippet of 5 lb. Virtually any of the larger nymphs will work – lures are banned. Colour is more important than pattern and I use yellow, bright orange, white, or black. Fish the retrieve in sharp jerks, and be sure to watch for that last-minute crash take near your feet. I always make a point of looking for my fly before attempting to lift off for the next cast, and have had more than a few last-minute takers. Don't be afraid, just because it is a nymph, to whip that fly back on a fast retrieve: the trout are quite capable of catching it, and you'll miss fewer takes.

Summer

Weed growth will be more prolific, and you will see more through the water because of the higher elevation of the sun. Use a floating line, and keep it lighter – a No. 6 is ample – but make sure that the leader tippet is not less than 5 lb for weighted-nymph work. If you cannot get a take in the early morning, remember that many anglers adjourn to the pub between 12.30 and 2. It only takes half an hour with no anglers on the water for those 'uncatchable' trout to regain their confidence. A dry fly or surface buzzer fished on a slow retrieve will bring them on. Green is a favourite colour at Avington, so try Green Buzzers, or tie up a standard Pheasant Tail pattern in a green. For the weighted-nymph work on bigger fish, try patterns like Green Beast, Mayfly, and Hare's Ear.

Avington doesn't really have a good rise of flies to make surface activity predominant, even in the late-summer evenings, but they do get the 'Fisherman's Curse' or smuts that drive you crazy. Although they were previously thought to be a waste of time, I have still taken the odd trout on tiny weighted nymphs. But you must be prepared to make a single accurate cast about 2 ft in front of a 'smutting' trout. Pause for a second after the cast, then start the retrieve by 'figure-of-eighting' the line into your hand.

Autumn

One of the best times for the centre and lower lakes is the autumn. The Damsel nymph will be the killing pattern, and I would suggest fishing it on an intermediate Airflo No. 8 line. That way you can start it back straight away for a surface-feeding trout, or making a longer leading cast in front of the fish, pausing for a few more seconds before you make the retrieve. Any trout previously pricked and lost may not be powering around as they would in the summer.

Look for stationary trout near the deeper banks, alongside a weedbed, or near an overhanging bush. Drop the fly about 3 ft away from them and watch their response. If the pectoral fins start to paddle about and quiver, then start the retrieve in pausing, snatchy jerks. Watch for that mouth to open and close before you lift the rod into a strike. Other good flies are the Black Aggravator, the Stick Fly, and the Montana Nymph. As a basic guide, if the weather is blustery and destroying your vision, stick to either end of any of the three lakes. That way you will still be in a good holding area.

Winter

This is not my favourite season, even at Avington. Many anglers will still be using the floating lines, with the nymph in the first few inches of water. I like to fish a faster sink through the deep holes, letting the line rest on the bottom, but lightly greasing the leader and using a buoyant fly to ride above any remaining weed. A long, steady pull is all that you need as a retrieve. Takes can be incredibly soft, so increase the speed of your pull if you feel any dragging. Often it turns out to be a nice rainbow! Any pattern of nymph will do, but I believe in just three colours: black, orange, and white. I see no need to mix all three colours into the one pattern in an attempt to make the ultimate fly. It rarely succeeds, so try them as single colours, and vary the speed of retrieve rather than change the pattern. Deep and slow is usually the watchword for winter fishing on most waters.

GENERAL INFORMATION

Avington can be fished by advance booking only, and there are no half-days available in principle. However, if you ring at the last minute, Roy will check the bookings and if it is a quiet day he may just give you a half-day ticket. But I warn you: it gets very hard after about 11 AM, by which time many of the fish have been caught. Finishing time is sunset or 8.30 PM, whichever is earlier. The rod limit on all three lakes and the river should be around twenty, and the day-ticket price of £20.00 is for four fish from the lakes and two from the river. Roy also sells season and half-season rods. There is a toilet, a car park, and a refreshment lodge. No spectators or dogs are allowed.

For more information contact: Roy Ward, Avington Trout Fishery Avington, Nr. Itchen Abbas, Winchester, Hants. SO21 1BZ. Telephone: (096278) 312.

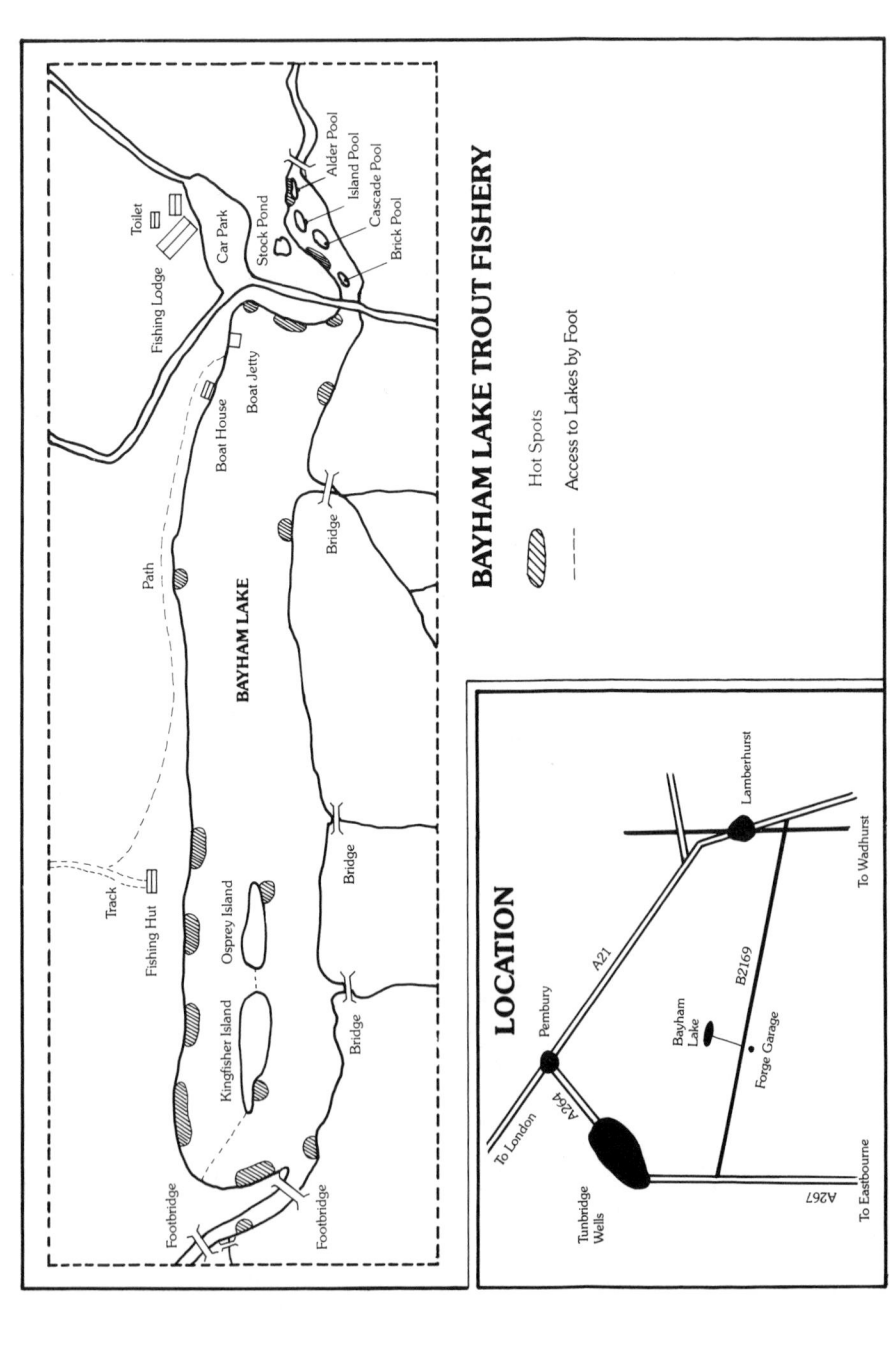

BAYHAM LAKE

When it comes to running a trout fishery to near perfection, John Parkman's Bayham Lake fishery, in Kent, must come out on top. John treats everybody as an equal and is genuinely delighted when an excited fisherman climbs the steps to the hut in order to weigh in a good fish. As far as I can remember, I have never drawn a blank at this water, and if you want a real shot at nice-condition fish in pleasant surroundings, then Bayham is certainly worth a visit. Of course all waters have their 'off' days, but ring John a day or so beforehand and you will get the most detailed analysis you could want.

As a place to take the family it ranks as ideal, for any non-fishing visitors can sit in the car park high over the lake and see where the action is taking place. The countryside around the fishery is exceptionally attractive, being part of the High Weald, designated an area of Outstanding Natural Beauty. There are a number of places of interest in the vicinity, including Lamberhurst vineyard, the ruins of the medieval Bayham Abbey, the ancient spa town of Tunbridge Wells, Scotney Castle, and the many old and beautiful Wealden villages. All these provide more than enough to fill the day for the family and are especially pleasant in the days of high summer.

Bayham Lake is large enough to take some 30–40 anglers before it could be considered overcrowded. Its location in the heart of the countryside on a private estate ensures that air of seclusion that the discerning fly fisherman looks for in his pursuit of first-class sport with big trout. The origin of the lake is interesting in that it was created in the 17th century by drawing on the River Teise, as a 'hammer' pond, to provide a source of power for the great iron forge of Bayham. This was located where the cascades now stand and is reputed to have produced many of the cannon for Nelson's ships at the Battle of

Trafalgar. Subsequently the lake was enlarged as part of the land-scaping carried out by the illustrious landscape gardener Humphrey Repton when he laid out the park for the first Marquis of Camden. The lake was then stocked with coarse fish and remained as an ornamental water and coarse fishery until the late 1970s.

John Parkman acquired the lake in 1978, by which time it was in a state of severe neglect. Dredging and other preparatory work took nearly two years, and the water opened as a trout fishery in the spring of 1980. Initial stocking was with brown, rainbow, and brook trout, and the stocking policy provided for a high percentage of very large fish. Since 1986, all replenishment has been done with rainbow trout bought only from the best restocking fish farms and averaging around 2½ lb.

As a rough guide to just how productive this fishery can be, the final statistics for 1987 make very impressive and interesting reading. Early March, when the fishery opens, sometimes give cool, dry weather. This happened in 1987, and as this weather lasted through March it gave Bayham the best start to a season since 1980, with an excellent stock of overwintered triploid rainbows feeding avidly and fighting superbly. The new season's stock settled in early and soon rivalled the overwintered stock for condition and fighting abilities. All that spring and summer there were long periods of excellent fishing conditions, which were reflected in a remarkable catch rate.

When October came, however, the weather showed just how perverse it can be, delivering two weeks of continuous rain, followed by the devastating hurricane of the night of the 15th. This great storm totally destroyed the fishing lodge, and devastated the surrounding parkland, bringing down forever many of the superb specimen trees which surround the lake. The remainder of the season was something of a trial for both the working parties who assisted John, and the fishermen, who had to operate from a temporary shed.

The back-end fishing came good and at least rivalled the previous two years. A staggering total of 13,422 rainbows were landed by 5306 rods, easily exceeding the target of 12,500 for one season. The number of specimen fish (those in excess of 3 lb) increased by some 22 per cent from 1342 to 1644, with a boom also in the real heavyweights recorded. In all, 912 fish between 3 lb and 4 lb were

If you get tired of bank fishing at Bayham, then manager John Parkman can provide you with a boat to fish the centre of the main lake. This can be particularly useful in high summer, when sport from the bank gets harder.

taken, 294 over 4 lb, 212 over 5 lb, 108 over 6 lb, 58 over 7 lb, 35 over 8 lb, 12 over 9 lb, 8 over 10 lb, 2 over 11 lb, and one each over 12, 13, and 14 lb. The Merrydown Trophy for the best fish of the season was won by Norman Rowles of Gravesend, with a rainbow trout of 14 lb 8 oz taken on a size 12 Yellow Montana, 4 lb leader, and a floating line. Mr Rowles also created a new fishery bag record with five fish for a total weight of 27 lb 8 oz, and to his credit this did not include his biggest fish. The record rainbow for Bayham weighed in at a whopping 17 lb 9 oz and was taken in May 1984.

APPROACH AND TACKLE

There must be something to suit the style of virtually any angler at Bayham. You can cast a line from the dam into the deeper water, or stalk an individual fish in the confines of the Teise itself. How about judging your talent by trying to extract a rainbow on an upstream nymph from one of the cascade pools? Or you can hire a boat and drift down the middle of the lake, casting a dry fly or surface nymph at any rising fish.

Suitable tackle for the fishery is normally an 8½ ft or 9 ft rod, rated 5/7 and paired with the appropriate weight of line. Long leaders are recommended, with a tippet strength of not less than 5 lb breaking strain. Long casting can be an advantage from certain pitches, so it is wise to pack a weight-forward No. 7 line for this use.

Although a large body of water – sixteen acres – for what I still term a 'small' water, Bayham is relatively shallow. For this reason alone it is probably best fished with a floating line. The majority of the rainbows will come in the top 18 in of water, and if a greater depth is required this can be achieved by the use of a longer leader and a leaded nymph. I use mostly larger nymph patterns with a good underbody of lead strips. Season times are from mid-March to mid-December, and if it should be cold at the beginning or end of the season a sinking line may be used. I use the Airflo intermediates or slow sinks, finding the depth required by coupling them with a longer leader and a heavily leaded nymph. Small lures are allowed, but don't automatically couple them with fast-sink lines, because they can be even more effective fished on or near the surface.

Always make sure you fish your fly right to the moment you lift it from the water. When coarse fish fry are present, the rainbows of Bayham's main lake will harry them right in to the edge. The thinking angler will cast his fly along the bankside, rather than straight out.

The lake bed slopes evenly from west to east and is approximately 4 ft deep at the western end, and 9 ft at the eastern end. As for weedbeds, there is nothing of prominence that may provide difficult conditions or create an overabundance of insect life. As the lake lies virtually east–west in a fairly steep valley, the best of the fishing comes when there is a gentle westerly airflow and an overcast sky. Surprisingly, a light easterly wind often produces excellent fishing from the dam. This is well worth noting, as a wind that is even partly from the east will generally reduce the catch rate at most other venues. As the lake is fed by the Teise, the worst conditions are produced by heavy, continuous rain, which can colour the water badly and make the fishing almost impossible for two or three days. However, reasonable rainfall in the dog days of high summer can produce a flush of fresh water that sometimes puts the trout in a feeding mood. Again, I advise phoning John first to check existing conditions, especially if there has been heavy rain over a long period. Another attraction of Bayham is the chance to sample the river fishing, as there is a mile of double-bank fishing incorporating the series of waterfalls and pools which are downstream from the lake and are highly prolific.

SEASONAL TACTICS

Spring

There should be plenty of over wintered triploid rainbows moving, so unless the mid-March opening proves very cold, an Intermediate or floating line will suffice. Small lures like the Viva, Appetiser, or Baby Doll will produce fish for those using sinking lines. Use a Montana nymph, Damsel, or Mayfly for floating or sunk leaders. Keep your retrieve speed fairly slow, and watch for the fly to appear in your vision before lifting off for a recast. The dam area is particularly productive in early spring.

Summer

This is the prime time for taking those fish swimming just below the surface, and the topwater man will find sport with the main hatches of midges, mayflies, damsel flies, hawthorns, and sedges. Early morning on the cascades and pools can be really productive with all of these patterns, and from here you can either graduate up the Teise to stalk individual fish, or move to the main lake for standard nymph fishing. If you stay until dusk, and I advise this on those sultry summer evenings, try a buzzer fished slowly through the surface film on a figure-of-eight retrieve. Don't make the mistake of thinking small fish take only small flies. A five-pounder will sometimes tear that roll of line straight from your hands, so make sure you don't break the fish off as you lift into him.

Autumn

This is a good time for fishing the surface either from the boat or from around the edges of Kingfisher and Osprey islands. It is also worth noting that from early October very large late-evening hatches of the Great Sedge sometimes occur, so that at such times the fishing around sunset can be very productive indeed. The dry fly enthusiast can make his own judgement on fly patterns, but the Brown or Silver Sedge, Black Gnat, or White Moth should all be tried. If you fish beneath the surface, try a Montana nymph for at least an hour, but make sure it has a green thorax. Also try a black or red buzzer. Surface fishing can be good from both the dam and the cascades at this time of year.

Winter

Given a mild November and December, the fishing will be almost as productive as the rest of the year. The trend will be towards small lures fished on slow-sink lines and 10 ft leaders, with a tippet strength of not less than 5 lb. Patterns to start with are Jack Frost, Appetiser, Viva, and Baby Doll. Another productive method I have found is to use a sunk line, but grease the leader so that the lure doesn't pick up the dead leaves on the bottom. With the fly suspended above the bottom debris you can slow your retrieve right down. Winter is the time to try your own patterns, and don't be afraid to experiment a little.

GENERAL INFORMATION

This fishery is possibly the most professionally run water I know and includes a range of facilities for the fly fisherman. There is a tackle shop in the fishing lodge, from which all the necessary accessories are available, but not rods, reels, and fly lines. There are over two hundred fly patterns and so there is no worry about not being able to lay your hands on a popular local pattern. Tackle can also be hired and costs just £2.00 per day for rod, reel, and line. Leaders and flies cost extra. A fully qualified instructor is available by appointment, and his charge is £10.00 per hour for individual tuition.

Regulations on the fishery are as follows. Day and half-day permits allow you to fish from 7.30 AM until dusk. Season permit holders may start at sunrise, which is great if you want to capitalize on high-summer sport. Rod numbers are limited to 45 per day, and advance booking of both boats and permits is advised. All fishing is with artificial fly only. No hook larger than a size 10 long shank may be used. Lures and wet flies may be used on the lake, but fishing on the cascade pools and on the Teise upstream from the lake is limited to dry fly and nymph. Any nymph used in these areas must be a recognized imitation of a natural food item. When boat fishing, trolling with the flies dragging behind the boat is not allowed, and wading from the shore is also forbidden. All trout caught must be killed. The number of trout which may be taken without extra payment is shown on the permit. Rods who have killed their permitted quota may buy a second permit, or may continue fishing on the original permit and pay, at the current rate per pound deadweight, for all additional fish up to a maximum of eight. Under no circumstances may a permit holder exceed the absolute catch limit of eight fish in any one session. Make sure you put details of your catch in the fishery log book, as this ensures that restocking will be accurate. No dogs are allowed, and children under the age of twelve are not admitted. Cars may be parked only in the car park, and fishermen casting from the dam must exercise care towards vehicles and people passing behind.

The range of permit prices for 1989 is as follows. All prices are exclusive of VAT.

Full-day rod (7.30 AM-dusk): £23.00 for a five-fish limit
Half-day rod (7.30 AM-2 PM or 2 PM-dusk): £13.00 for a three-fish limit

Newsreader Leonard Parkin looks delighted with this 7 lb Bayham rainbow, landed during a promotional tournament. Fish this size, and very much larger, are by no means rare in either the main lake or the cascade pools.

Boat: Full day: £8.00 single, £12.00 double; half day: £5.00 single, £8.00 double

The system of season rods is fairly complex in comparison to that of other fisheries, but consists of a basic season permit made up of 10 units, i.e. 10 full or half days. Each basic permit carries one extra unit free, thus providing 11 fishing sessions on this permit. For those seeking more fishing than these basic permits provide, additional sessions can be added in multiples of five units, and each additional group of five units carries one extra unit free of charge. The system is shown below, and carries obvious financial advantages if you fish a lot.

10 × half days (giving 11 full days): £149.00 for a three-fish limit.
15 × half days (giving 17 half days): £224.25 for a three-fish limit.
20 half days (giving 23 half days): £299.00 for a three-fish limit.
10 × full days (giving 11 full days): £230.00 for a five-fish limit.
15 × full days (giving 17 full days): £345.00 for a five-fish limit.
20 full days (giving 23 full days): £460.00 for a five-fish limit.

For unlimited access and fishing, speak to John, who will doubtless be delighted to give you a price. There you have as much information as you require to enjoy a day at Bayham. The fact that John saw over 5000 rods at his fishery during 1987 must surely indicate that the water is well worth a visit.

For more information contact: John Parkman, Bayham Lake Trout Fishery, Bayham Abbey, Lamberhurst, Tunbridge Wells, Kent TN3 8BG. Telephone: (0892) 890276.

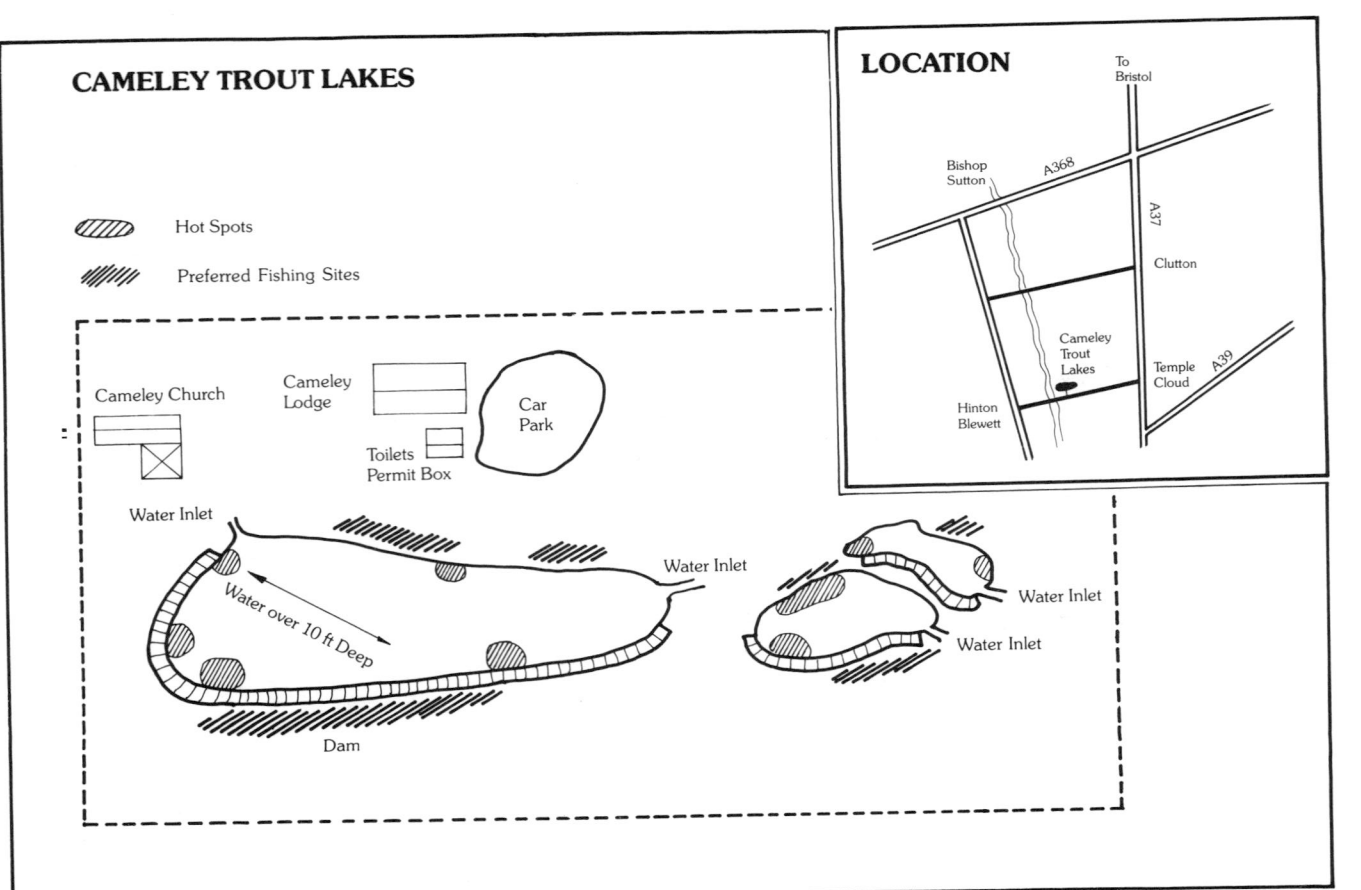

CAMELEY TROUT LAKES

◖░░░◗ Hot Spots

▨▨▨ Preferred Fishing Sites

Cameley Church

Cameley Lodge

Toilets
Permit Box

Car Park

Water Inlet

Water over 10 ft Deep

Water Inlet

Water Inlet

Water Inlet

Dam

LOCATION

To Bristol

Bishop Sutton

A368

A37

Clutton

Cameley Trout Lakes

Temple Cloud

A39

Hinton Blewett

CAMELEY

To the untrained eye, a lot of the smaller trout venues seem to be the same. Yet each one has something that makes it a little special. In the case of Cameley Trout Lakes, near Bristol, it has to be the location, for the beautiful Somerset countryside is a pleasure to behold. The owner, Mr John Harris, is also a farmer, and formed the first lake by diverting the tiny River Cam to avoid farm pollution. This drained the surrounding land and the main lake came into being in 1974. This single lake was first stocked with trout in 1976, and two other lakes have since been formed. All three lakes are situated upstream from the old Priory.

Cameley was the first small water trout venue to open in the area. Just across the Mendips lies Chew Valley Reservoir, a famed quality trout reservoir that has long supplied the bigwater fisherman of Bristol and the surrounding area with their best sport. Now some of these same anglers visit Cameley to try their hand at a water a fraction of the size of the vast Chew Valley. Cameley boasts both browns and rainbows, either of which is capable of putting a healthy bend in the rod. The three lakes total five acres and two of them are stocked with rainbow trout between 1 lb 8 oz and 7 lb. The other lake is stocked with browns only, but they are generally in great condition and range in weight from 1 lb 8 oz to 5 lb, ensuring good sport for fishermen of all shapes and sizes.

Apart from water from the tiny River Cam, all the lakes are fed by springs which have their beginning in the Mendips. Since fishing began, the water quality has been so good that weed blooms have ballooned during the hot summer months. The lakes are now being excavated to a depth averaging around 8 ft, which, it is hoped, will minimize weed growth. Although the idea of first having a lake was to provide wildfowl shooting, a water authority engineer was quick to point out that the quality of such liquid gold would be wasted on wildfowling and was far better suited to trout.

The record rainbow at Cameley weighed in at 11 lb 7 oz, and the brown trout record is 5 lb 8 oz. It is more a personal fishery than a big, high-intensity, water, and the relevant statistics are accordingly lower. In 1987, 605 fishermen visited the venue and accounted for 1568 trout. The heaviest rainbow of that season fell to a Bristol angler and topped 9 lb. All three lakes are stocked twice weekly with fish from 1 lb 12 oz upwards, from the fishery's own stock ponds. This gives the stock time to get acclimatized and to start a regular diet on the insect life. The lush green weed growth, although possibly a problem for sunk-line anglers, means there will still be plenty of insect life about.

APPROACH AND TACKLE

The best way to fish Cameley is with a floating line, sunk leader, and unleaded fly. You may be surprised at just how shallow a rainbow will come in his quest for a properly presented fly. Before the recent deepening, the chemical Clarisan was used as a weed-growth inhibitor, with no detrimental effect on the fish. The smaller top lake is best when fished early on, as it is very sheltered and the water temperature can be a little higher. However, this higher temperature also promotes earlier weed growth, and it is for this reason that I recommend fishing this lake in the first couple of months of the season. After that, try the main lake, concentrating your efforts on the deeper water near the dam. Fishing times are from sunrise to sunset.

Fishing is by dry fly, nymph, and small wet fly (size 14). There is an overall length limit of 1 in on all patterns. This measurement is taken from the eye of the hook to the end of the fly dressing. The most popular fly patterns at Cameley are the traditionals like Black and Peacock Spider, Butcher, March Brown, Pheasant Tail nymph, Stick Fly, and buzzers. The five acres can all be covered from either bank, so line sizes can be kept light and there is no need for shooting heads. Correspondingly, rods over 9 ft long are not necessary. Fishing tackle can be hired by advance booking. Line sizes should be double

If you don't want to look for a big trout, you can spend your time catching the standard-size rainbows as this local youngster did. The fishing is enhanced by the view and seclusion of the valley, as well as by the limit on rod numbers.

tapered size 5/7 and rods should be 8½–9 ft. The strength of the leader can be as much as 6 lb, although a 3 lb leader will give you more takes.

SEASONAL TACTICS

Spring

Try the smaller top lake first, which may be a little warmer and make the trout more active in the early weeks. Slow-sink lines with any of the traditional wet flies fished on a fairly sharp retrieve will get the most takes. Wet flies are usually associated with river fishing, but many patterns are highly successful on early spring lakes. There may even be the chance of taking a few fish off the surface with unweighted nymphs like Pheasant Tail.

Summer

The most pleasant fishing is in the summer, when you can fish 2 ft down for browns using weighted shrimp patterns, or use a floating line fished slowly across the surface for rainbows, generally in the main lake. Early morning will see Mayfly, Damsel, and similar nymphs proving most popular. Remember to take it easy during the middle of the day: take a light lunch in the restaurant and then renew your attack with either dry fly or buzzers in the early evening. The prime fishing times are early and late.

Autumn

Stick with the floating line, but extend your leader length to at least 10 ft in order to keep to a minimum the disturbance to a taking fish. Make your casts easy and clean, covering as much of the water as you can, searching out the fish. That way you have less chance of spooking any trout by thrashing the water to oblivion. Almost any pattern will produce – it is entirely up to the individual – but nymphs with green, black, or red in them get the most pulls.

GENERAL INFORMATION

As well as providing great surface fishing, the Harris family own a

An angler prepares to net a very big rainbow, while the owners of the fishery, John Harris and his son, watch with interest. In the background are the converted farm buildings that now include a fine restaurant.

restaurant, recently extended to cater for over 100 guests, so that you can spend the morning fishing and then have lunch while overlooking the main lake at the bottom of the pasture. Of course a gourmet would not drop his food to rush down to the water's edge on seeing a trout rise – but an angler just might! If you want to spend a weekend there with the family, the lodge can take care of your every need. The farm buildings from which the present lodge was converted are now scarcely recognizable as such .The old bull pen is now the lounge, the barn and stables are the restaurant, and the hayloft is the bedroom area. The attention to detail in creating the lodge and restaurant has also inspired the conversion of the old cow shed into a Georgian-style bungalow. Named Barton Springs from the nearby spring that fills a pool, this bungalow is available for renting, and overlooks the dam end of the lake. It takes seven anglers, and splitting the cost of the hire between a group makes a weekend's trouting there very attractive indeed.

Opening day is on 1 March and ticket prices are as follows:

Day ticket £12.00 (four-fish limit).
Half-day ticket £8.00 (two-fish limit).

For more information contact: John Harris, Cameley Trout Lakes, Hillcrest Farm, Temple Cloud, Nr Bristol BS18 5AQ. Telephone: (0761) 52423.

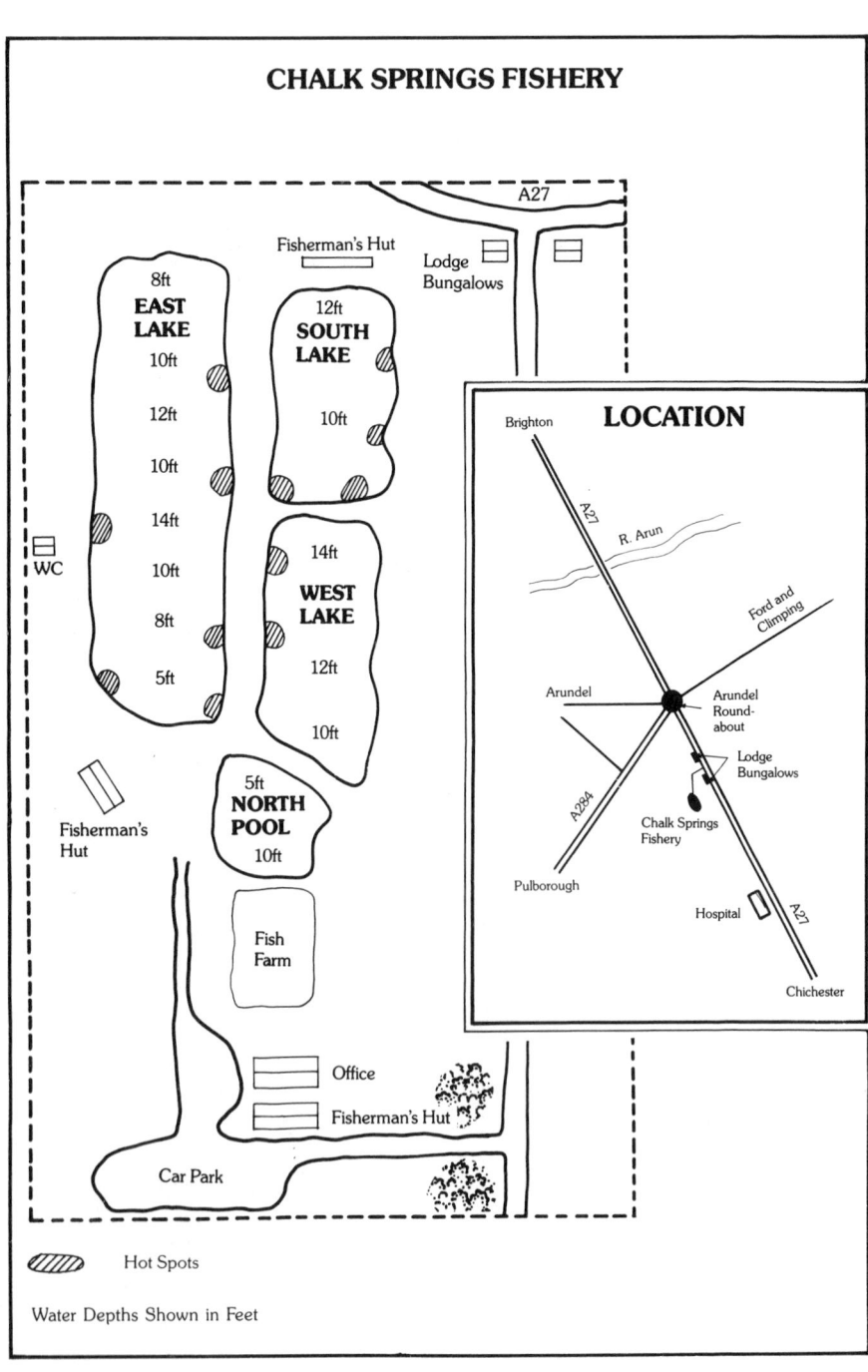

CHALK SPRINGS FISHERY

A27

Fisherman's Hut

Lodge Bungalows

EAST LAKE
8ft
10ft
12ft
10ft
14ft
10ft
8ft
5ft

SOUTH LAKE
12ft
10ft

WC

WEST LAKE
14ft
12ft
10ft

NORTH POOL
5ft
10ft

Fisherman's Hut

Fish Farm

Office

Fisherman's Hut

Car Park

LOCATION

Brighton

A27

R. Arun

Ford and Climping

Arundel

Arundel Round-about

Lodge Bungalows

A284

Chalk Springs Fishery

Pulborough

Hospital

A27

Chichester

///// Hot Spots

Water Depths Shown in Feet

CHALK SPRINGS

Trout waters that rarely freeze up during the winter must surely be at a premium. I know of only one such venue myself and that is Chalk Springs Fishery in Sussex, managed by Jonathan Glover. Situated on the Duke of Norfolk's Estate near Arundel, it is one of the easiest waters to find as it is only a short distance from the main Arundel roundabout. Chalk Springs is ideal for a family day out, since while the angler gets his fishing hours in, the family can disappear onto the South Downs or look around Arundel, which has historic significance with its castle, its Cathedral, the Wildfowl Trust and other tourist attractions. The castle is in fact the seat of the Duke of Norfolk, whose eldest son, the Earl of Arundel, is a partner in the fishery.

The South Downs form the basis of the surrounding chalk grounds that give rise to the name of the fishery and also account for the superb clarity of the water. I was amazed, on being shown the fishery photo album by Jonathan, at the amount of work that had been put into the landscaping. Originally reclaimed from marshy scrubland, the area had stood for some fifty years as watercress beds until 1984, when the excavations were completed and the water was stocked. One of the problems with the excavations was that the springs were so prolific in providing water that the digging machines kept getting bogged down. Slowly the digging was completed, giving a depth range of around 4 ft down to 15 ft. This has created four lakes all of which are basically quite small, but which, combined, would total several acres.

Jonathan recorded his best-ever season in 1987, with a good range of fish from 2 lb right up to double figures. The average catch figure of 2.7 fish shows the productiveness of the water, and the fishery record for both species of trout is enviable. Rainbows of up to 11 lb have been landed, as well as browns of up to 9 lb 1 oz. It is the latter species which I find particularly interesting, simply because you find fewer fisheries about today that house big brownies. The stock ponds have a selection of superb browns over 5 lb, and in one season Jonathan recorded no fewer than thirty browns in excess of 4 lb, with the others averaging around 2 lb 8 oz. Browns are generally thought to take better in the deep water during the winter, and you can visit Chalk Springs in the knowledge that it is unlikely to be frozen. One night they even recorded 12 degrees of frost, yet still no ice formed on the lakes.

APPROACH AND TACKLE

The three main lakes are deceptively deep, dropping to 12 ft or so, and you may find some difficulty in gauging just how close to a cruising trout to drop your weighted nymph. As the trout run deeper your fly will just not be down at their depth, and because of the clarity of the water they will appear to be swimming a lot shallower than they really are. The constant flow of spring water, along with its 'anti-freeze' qualities, ensures that the weed will be there throughout the winter months. Standard nymph patterns can still be used with some enthusiasm. As the venue is surrounded by trees, there can be considerable activity with the Hawthorn fly. There is a strict ban on the use of lures and fly size is limited to a size 10 long-shank hook — just a single, as no droppers are allowed.

With lures out of the way you can concentrate on dry fly or leaded nymphs. Popular patterns for the dry fly enthusiast are Daddy Longlegs, Mayfly, Hawthorn, and Sedges. For weighted nymphs you have the Gold Ribbed Hare's Ear, Pheasant Tail nymph, Montana, Damsel and Mayfly nymphs. The months of April and May are usually the most popular with surface men as the hawthorn and mayfly can occur together then. For that reason it can often be worth just sitting and waiting for some rises. Since the waters are quite small and popular, the trout soon get used to lines criss-crossing them. But by resting an area you give the trout the confidence to start taking notice of the insect life rather than darting from weedbed to weedbed in an effort to avoid the angler.

Watch for a rise, although because of the clear water you will probably see the fish anyway. Select your casting distance carefully and make your first cast count. You will derive a great deal of satisfaction from taking a fish like this, for the approach is far more rewarding than standard nymphing. It may also pay you to try one or more of the following patterns throughout the day: Governor, Green Latex Grub, and Black Pennell. The latter is one of the best for fishing during the middle of the day, when the fish have usually become more wary. The basic advice about wind direction is the same as for many other waters. Any easterly wind is awkward, putting the trout off, although I still recommend perseverance, particularly in the early morning and evening. A wind with south or west in it that puts a slight ripple on the surface will see your catch rate rise.

As a guide to maximum depths, the following is fairly accurate: the north pool drops away to 10 ft, the west lake to 14 ft, the south lake 12 ft, and the larger east lake to 14 ft. The figures are for the centre in each case. I mention these depths simply because if you are interested in locating big brown trout, the deeper holding pools might just be of paramount importance. If a brownie is hooked and lost, or pricked by a hook, it retains the memory of that encounter for longer than the rainbow. It will repair to the deepest corner of any lake until it has regained some confidence to feed.

As Chalk Springs is only a small fishery, you need not use a rod longer than 10 ft, and 9 ft is easier to handle. For the same reason line ratings need only be 4/5 double tapers, or 6/7 if you need to overline slightly to aid casting. Leader tippet strength should be 6 lb to start with, dropping down to 3 lb when you are surface nymphing or fishing a dry fly during the late spring, early summer, and early autumn.

SEASONAL TACTICS

Spring

Nymph fishing using a fast-sink or slow-sink line and a heavily weighted nymph will score best. If you must use a floating line, make sure you have a long leader, and fish fly patterns like the Montana, Aggravator, or Mayfly nymph. For the surface fly fisherman there will be action on buzzers and Hawthorn. The fast-sink man will be well advised to watch for those last-minute crash takes from brown trout, and he should bear in mind that they will most likely be over 3 lb, and possibly up to 8 lb.

Summer

All of the standard nymph fishing techniques will produce, with either slow-sink, Intermediate, or floating line and patterns like Mayfly, Damsel, Montana, Gold Ribbed Hare's Ear, or Pheasant Tail nymph. For dry fly, try experimenting with the Daddy Longlegs, Mayfly, Hawthorn, and Sedge patterns. Particularly successful, and certainly satisfying, is the stalking of individual trout using any weighted shrimp patterns. But remember that clarity of water and the good depth. If you tie your own shrimp patterns, include plenty of lead in the dressing to make them get down quickly.

Brown trout are big at Chalk Springs. Manager Jonathan Glover has plenty of high-quality browns in his stock ponds, put into the lakes to 'spice up' the fishing. More fisheries now seem to be adding just a few browns to their regular stock to give the fisherman a bonus.

Autumn

Tactics for the autumn can be almost the same as for spring. Although many anglers feel lost without the use as a back-up of traditional fry-imitating lures, just use a big nymph pattern and fish it faster than you would normally. The Daddy Longlegs fished dry is also good.

Winter

In winter Chalk Springs is one of the better fisheries. All nymph fishing will catch at this time of year, so put away your floating lines and stick to the slow-sink or fast-sink, moving round each lake until you pull a fish. Although lures are banned, Jonathan will allow very small patterns to be used during the winter, when insect movement may be almost nil.

GENERAL INFORMATION

Both tackle and fishing instruction can be arranged, but do give Jonathan a ring in advance so that he can organize it. No tackle is sold, but you can pick up a few leaders and flies on the fishery. There is ample parking, an office, a fisherman's hut, and toilets.

Opening hours are from 9 AM until dusk. Rainbow trout can be fished every day of the year, and brown trout from 3 April to 31 October. Ticket prices are as follows:

Day ticket: £17.00 (four-fish limit); £13.00 (three-fish limit).

Season tickets are open to negotiation with Jonathan, and he also offers an incentive to any bulk or club bookings. Access to the fishery is just off the Arundel roundabout on the A27 Brighton to Chichester road.

For more information contact: Jonathan Glover, Chalk Springs Fishery, Park Bottom, Arundel, West Sussex. Telephone: (0903) 883742.

DEVER SPRINGS TROUT FISHERY

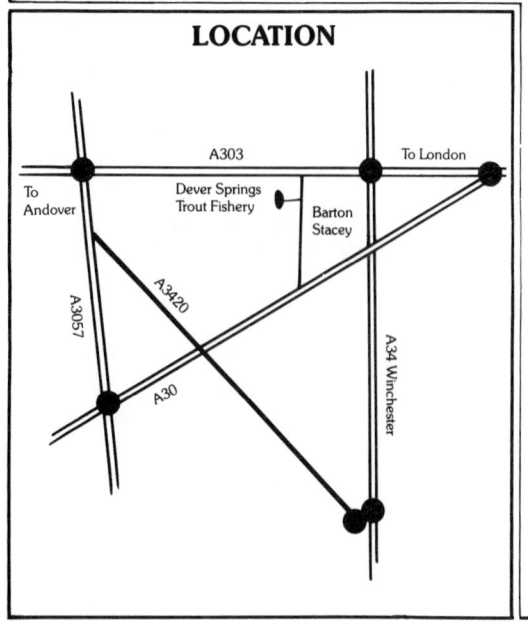

RIVER DEVER

SPRING LAKE

Stock Ponds

WILLOW LAKE

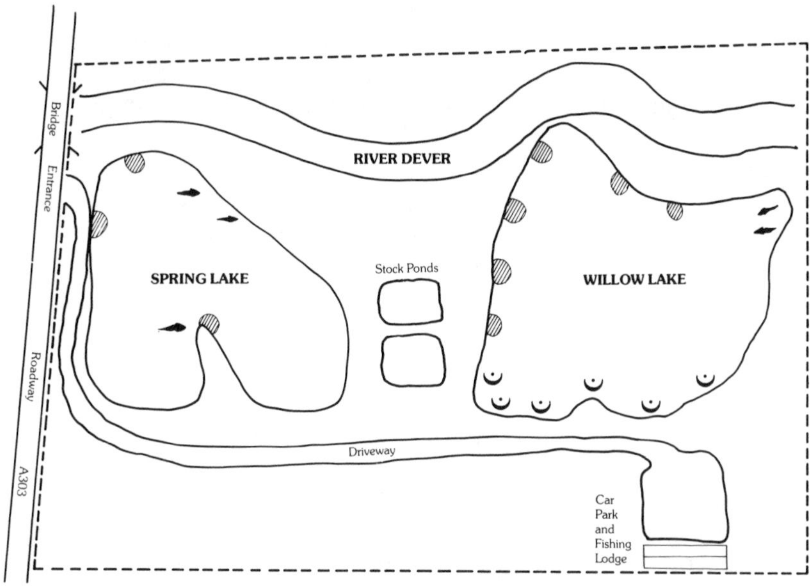

Bridge

Entrance

Roadway

A303

Driveway

Car
Park
and
Fishing
Lodge

LOCATION

A303

To London

To
Andover

Dever Springs
Trout Fishery

Barton
Stacey

A3057

A3420

A30

A34 Winchester

 Brown Trout

Stock Fish

Hot Spots

DEVER SPRINGS

As this book sets out to cover some of the top places to go trout fishing in the south, it cannot fail to include the venue most likely to set two new records. This information is red hot and by the time the book is at the printers I expect to see new records for both the rainbow and the brown trout. Dever Springs is located in a prime clean water area, and is fed by springs and the Dever, a tributary of the famous Test. Unlike many fisheries with their origins in gravel extraction workings, this venue was created purely with the fisherman in mind, and specializes in offering quality flyfishing, with a very real chance of taking a double-figure fish. The fishery owner Nigel Jackson and manager Andy Don take great care to bring their reared trout on to an excellent average size which few other waters can equal.

The venue was first started in 1984, when excavations were begun to reclaim much of the marshy land in order to transform it into a defined area of lake plus river. Previously, the Dever had run shallow the whole width of the ground, so that it was neccessary not only to build a new lake, but to push back the course of the river to its natural route and to build new banks with excavated gravel. The smaller Spring lake was the first to be started, followed by the construction of Willow lake. They couldn't be classified as large waters, with Spring at around 2 acres and Willow at 4 acres.

Half a mile or so of the Dever is also available, although few anglers leave the lakes to sample its sport. They could be missing out, for this tiny, clearwater stream offers the dedicated river flyfisher the chance of big grayling, and Nigel told me that he thinks they can top the British record for the species. I did sample the river there on my first trip and was amazed at the number of dark grayling drifting around in the fast current. My third cast at them saw a nice brown shoot out

Fishery manager Andy Don displays one of the author's brown trout landed from the River Dever which runs through the fishery. This fish was returned alive. The stream also holds some superb grayling, thought to be larger than the British record.

from a weedbed and attach itself to my fly. There are not many times when I curse a brown for snatching a fly from another fish, but those grayling were more important to me!

Both lakes are generally crystal clear and allow for the individual spotting of the bigger fish. Spring, being smaller and clearer, lends itself better to the capture of bigger trout. Willow is generally less clear, although as I write this, Spring has a slight bloom in it and Willow is the clear one! Fish them as you find them is all I can suggest. The lakes established themselves quickly, with the pure water yielding plenty of aquatic life and insects. Both lakes are stocked with top-quality brown and rainbow trout, and browns only are stocked in the river. The depths are uniform in spring, running fairly evenly at around 6½ ft all the way across. Willow is slightly deeper at about 10 ft, tapering off to 6½ ft, but with a tremendously large hole, where Nigel thinks many of the brownies must go. This is thought to be in excess of 50 ft deep and was caused by being at the extremity of the dragline bucket that emptied the ground.

Nigel firmly believes that if he is to offer anglers big fish, he must push them on from only the best fry. His fry come from Anna Valley Trout Farm, where a big hatchery operates, and they come in at about a hundred to the pound. He cannot hatch his own because the eggs need pure bore-hole water, and permission to sink bore holes is subject to strict conditions. For the present, he must push the trout weight up by intensive feeding. The fry are grown on in three different batches. The rainbows are pushed through in April and again in July, while the browns come only in November. He takes 10,000 each time, and hopes to push through his system up to 4000 browns and 20,000 rainbows each year.

The intensive feeding programme is unlike that of most other fisheries in that it has two stages. The stock is sorted to separate the fast growers from the standard fish, and the former are kept aside to be the big fish for the following year. Nigel aims to put the maximum amount of protein in his fish and, as well as automatic feeders, gives them food as fry up to nine times every day. To maintain his colossal growth rate he needs good water, quality stock fish from which to work, and the efforts of both himself and Andy.

As an indication of Nigel's productiveness, in 1987 he held 10,000 three-year-old fish of 3–8lb, which he pushes up into double-figure fish before the end of the following season. His best winter growth rate was achieved with stocks from Dave Riley, which he bought in at 6 oz on 20 August, and by 1 March the following year he had pushed them to over a kilo, or nearly 2¼ lb each. This is due to the fact that he can hold so many more fish with a high survival rate in the colder weather. Naturally, during the warm weather of summer, this figure drops, as fewer fish can be held in the same given area of stock pond. Even so, his summer growth rates can produce fish of 3 lb from ones of 6 oz in less than six months, although this is because they are kept in very deep stock ponds to stabilize water temperatures.

Nigel currently uses a specialized 8 mm pellet made for him by Paul's Agriculture. It is made up of 55 per cent protein and is bonded as a slow-sinking pellet to reach the fish swimming a bit deeper. Because of the carcinogens in some pellets, he has changed to a new pigmentation pellet which makes the trout's flesh pink. Many anglers think the best pink rainbows are caused by feeding them exclusively on shrimp, but now we know that it is the pigmentation in the pellet itself that causes this.

The massive throughput of fish is designed solely for Dever Springs, and only when there is a surplus will Nigel sell off stock fish to other waters. As an indication of the body of trout he keeps, in the summer he expects to hold 15 tons of fish, and in the colder water of winter, more suitable to the metabolism of rainbows, he holds up to 35 tons. Last season about 15,000 fish were landed by the anglers, and he hopes to operate his fishing day policy as follows, though of course this may change at any time. He plans to open on 3 April and offer fishing right through the season until 31 October. From then until the end of December he hopes to open at weekends, and thereafter until the following season on a Sunday-only basis.

Dever's reputation as a big fish water is illustrated by the fact that 1987 saw 350 double figure fish landed, which Nigel hopes to push to 400 in 1988. On the small stretch of river the record for brown trout is 5 lb 8 oz, for rainbow 9 lb 4 oz, while the grayling average 2 lb and there is possibly a British record fish there. The lakes have yielded a record brown of 15 lb 2 oz and a rainbow of 16 lb 12 oz. However, scheduled for June 1988 were two monster fish, both grown on to put the British record well and truly out of sight. Nigel hopes to get the rainbow up to 32 lb and the brown past 20 lb. If you visit Dever you see why they have a minimum leader ruling of 6 lb.

This angler holds a big brown trout. There are plenty of quality browns in both lakes at Dever, many over 3 lb and some up to double figures. Careful stalking and fly presentation are the answer to their capture.

SEASONAL TACTICS

With daily stocking, each day should see the same, or at least similar, methods of catching fish. But some suggestions still are useful.

Spring

Start with a sinking line, maybe an Airflo fast-sink, to search out the depths where the odd overwintered fish might be. Willow lake lends itself best to this. Any mini lure will suffice, but remember hook size is limited to a size 8, with a ban on dressings with an overall length of more than 1 in. As the waters warm in early May you can expect the hawthorn fly to give some surface activity, so fish shallower with a slow-sink line. Then comes the mayfly hatch, which is really prolific and lasts from around 25 May right through to 15 July, which is by far the longest mayfly season I know of.

Summer

Stay with the floating line, but use a fast-sink leader of the type offered by Burgess that can be impregnated with a sinking additive. This allows you to get a leaded fly down quickly to a bigger trout, should you spot it cruising about. You can still fish the surface layers by changing from a fast-sink to a slow-sink leader and using an unleaded fly. Small green and brown Pheasant Tail nymphs will produce, as will the Hawthorn fished dry. Top flies in the summer are the Montana and the American Eyed Damsel fly, which is currently the most popular with the regulars of Dever Springs.

Autumn

If the weather is warm I advise staying with a slow sink. Large bodies of deep water take a lot longer to cool down than people imagine, and a slow-sink Airflo allows you to fish right on the surface, or 3 ft down. Mini Baby Dolls, Black Aggravator, American Eyed Damsel, or even a heavily leaded Mayfly will catch in the autumn. Try both ends of the spectrum with your retrieve. Before changing depths or position, make three slow retrieves, drawing the line in carefully in a figure-of-eight. Then fishing at the same depth, whip it back fast like a lure, even when using standard nymphs. This can provoke a crash take, and although it may not work everytime, it oftens picks up those finicky fish. As a pointer, traditionalists always regard September as the premier month to winkle out the better brownies. I would only suggest changing to a faster sink line in October, when you should fish a buoyant fly just off the dying weeds.

A truly massive fish: the new British record brown trout being introduced to the large lake at Dever Springs by owner Nigel Jackson. Such a specimen costs a lot of money to rear and this fish represents 5½ years' work and care by Nigel.

GENERAL INFORMATION

There is an ample car park, toilets, smoking facilities (for your catch!) and a tackle shop is planned. Dever offers a comprehensive fly stock and tackle for hire, with or without casting tuition. Advance booking is required, as this water is obviously one of the most popular in the south.

Finally, the following fishery rules should be noted. Spring lake is for floating line and nymph patterns only, while any fly method is allowed on Willow. The fishery is covered by a Southern Water Authority block licence. Fishing times are from 8 AM until half an hour after sunset. (Times are displayed at the fishing lodge.) No rod sharing is allowed, or teams of flies. All fish caught must be killed if over 12 in. Trout under this length are to be returned. No dogs, even if left in cars, are permitted, and children must be accompanied by a responsible adult. On the river, dry and upstream nymph only can be used. Wading is prohibited. Maximum hook size is No. 12 for long-shank nymph hooks. Unless invited to do so, no angler must encroach on another, and the minimum space between anglers should be 15 yards. Landing nets *must* be carried. All anglers must sign the book and record their catch, even nil returns, in order to assist in stocking management.

1989 prices at Dever Springs are:

Day ticket: £30.00 (four-fish limit).
Half-day ticket: £24.00 (three-fish limit).
Evening ticket: £17.00 (two-fish limit).

Access to the fishery is easy. It is located six miles from Andover and three-quarters of a mile off the main A303 Andover to London road, with an M3 connection. For more information contact: Nigel Jackson, Dever Springs Trout Fishery, Barton Stacey, Nr. Andover, Hants. SO21 3NP. Telephone: (026472) 592.

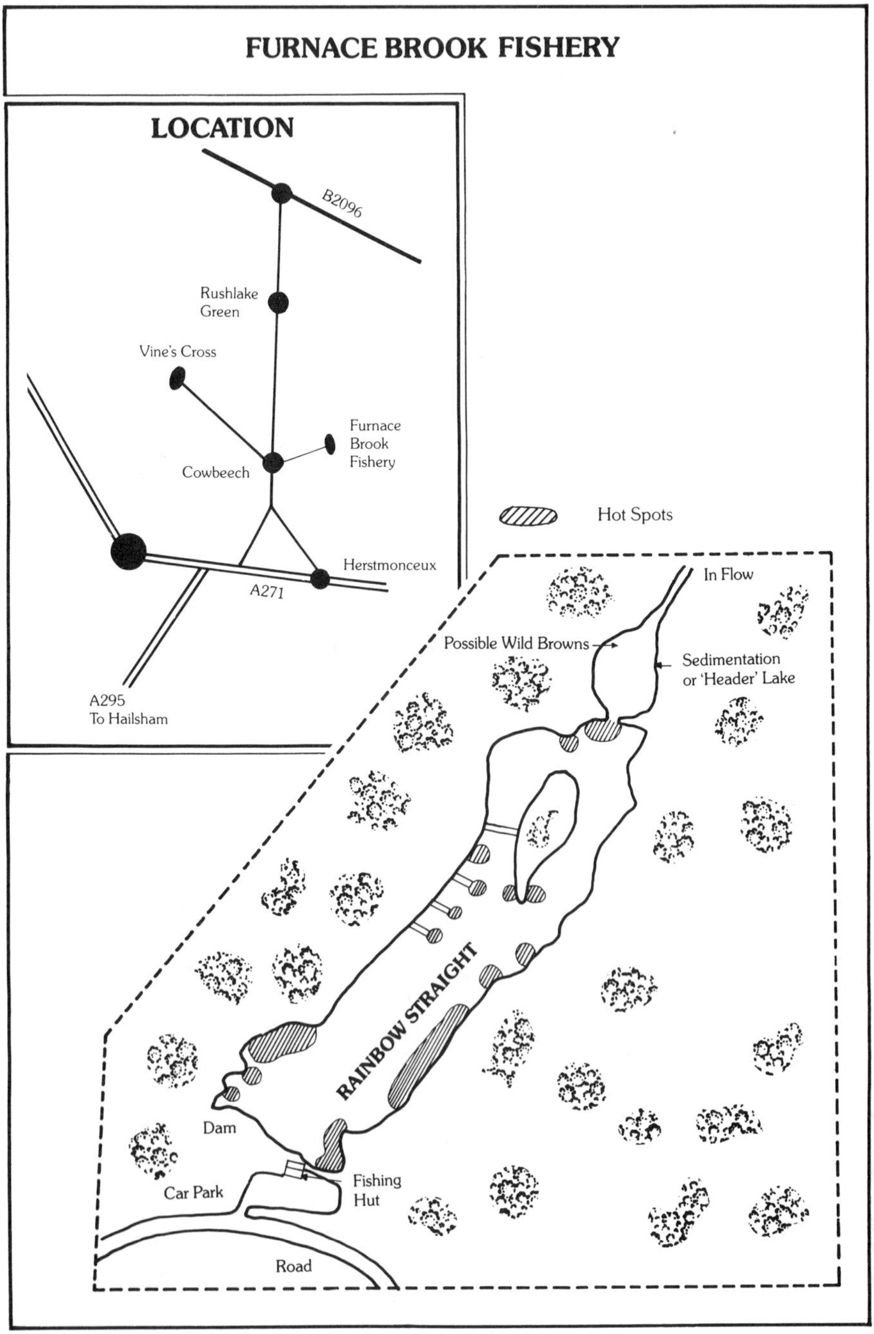

FURNACE BROOK FISHERY

LOCATION

B2096

Rushlake Green

Vine's Cross

Cowbeech

Furnace Brook Fishery

Herstmonceux

A271

A295 To Hailsham

Hot Spots

In Flow

Possible Wild Browns

Sedimentation or 'Header' Lake

RAINBOW STRAIGHT

Dam

Car Park

Fishing Hut

Road

FURNACE BROOK

This small water is to be found in a wooded valley just outside the town of Hailsham, in Sussex. It is amazing that you can drive off the busy A22 for just a few miles and be surrounded by the peace and quiet of this corner of the Sussex countryside. The fishery is owned by Laurence Ryan, a man who has a dear love of fishing, and who decided to opt out of the rat race and get into a business he could really enjoy. Previously he was a design engineer with the Ministry of Defence, and also looked after a trout fishery, working in this industry for some twelve years. He finally had more than he could stand of his high-pressure job and purchased Furnace Brook to transform it into the fishery and fish farm you will see today.

The lake itself, which is the backbone of the catchment area for the fish farm, was only a decade or so old, and had fallen into disrepair. Laurence's first job was to make good all the banking and to rebuild completely the sides of the stews. After carrying out extensive landscaping, he spent the next two years both establishing the venue as a true fishery and improving the production of the trout farm. Previously the commercial output of the fish farm had been a few table fish, but now Laurence claims to provide up to ten tons of rainbow trout for the table market in one year alone, as well as retaining enough trout to restock the fishing lake. Fish for the table are from about 12 oz up to 3 lb, while the mainstay fish for the lakes can run from 1 lb 4 oz up to 16 lb. Laurence also supplies about thirty other small enterprises with stocking rainbows.

Visitors to Furnace Brook may be surprised at the layout of the fish farm, as it is all located directly below the dam wall. Water is piped from the bottom of the centre of the lake, where the temperature is likely to remain constant, then fed into the four stock ponds, a five-ton double-raceway system which is under a poly-tunnel, and a

Koi carp farm. The poly-tunnel is a huge arched frame over a small lake, the entire area being covered with heavy-duty plastic sheeting. This maintains a constant temperature for his Koi carp, with water from 70 to 80° F (21–27° C) throughout the growing season. An interesting point about his Koi carp enterprise is the value of each individual fish. Depending on its coloration and the distribution of black marks, a fully grown Koi carp can change hands for . . . wait for it . . . up to £30,000. The most expensive specimen he has in his public display section is currently valued at some £7000. He grows about one million fry from eggs each year, and has even crossed mirror carp with Kois to produce what is known as a 'Ghost Koi'. He allows bored anglers who are not catching trout to take a look round the display units, but I expect any fisherman will want to see that £7000 fish nicknamed the 'Mary Rose'.

The fishing lake is about five acres in extent, and long and narrow. There is a small island at the far end. It was formed as a lake by damming the small feeder stream and letting the water back up against the side of the valley walls. Therefore if a lot of rain falls you can fish a water that has grown to six acres. But the rain can also prove something of a problem as it brings with it an incredible silt suspension washed down from the valley ditches above. The soil is a mixture of sandstone and clay, but the lakebed itself is entirely of clay.

If Laurence had not installed a special lake at the top of the fishery, the main lake would soon silt up. Situated at the inflow of the main lake and about 100 ft long and 70 ft wide, this lake is called the 'header' lake. It is really a sedimentation pond where all the silt in principle is trapped as sludge before it can get into the main lake. There is always water in the 'header' lake, and it is especially interesting to fly fishermen, as some of the rainbows stocked in the main lake will try to get up into the silt trap to taste the fresh water coming in with a flood. There are some browns in there too, which present a great challenge, since the fly must be placed with accuracy in the areas of shallow water close to natural cover.

The main lake is where most of your attention will be directed, especially as the 'header' lake can sludge up with 20 ft of silt in just 2½ years. The dam down by the fishing lodge will give you water to 20 ft in depth and it gets shallower the nearer you get to the back of

The main part of the lake at Furnace Brook is called 'Rainbow strait'. It is an excellent area for picking up the stockies, while the dam end offers the chance of larger fish.

the island, but even then it would be only a matter of a few feet nearer your feet that it slopes up. For the most part it will be about 9 ft deep, which gives you plenty of scope to use the full range of fly lines: floating, sinking, intermediate, and fast-sinking.

The stocking density is high – hardly surprising when Laurence has his own fish farm on tap. The catch average is about 11,000 fish a year, which breaks down into a rod average of 2.6 fish and an average size for rainbow of 2 lb 8 oz. Although he used to stock some browns, Laurence now replenishes fish taken with rainbows. Nevertheless, there are still some truly wild browns skulking about, and they are very big fish. Should you be fortunate enough to hook one – and takes don't come easy from any brown – then be prepared for fireworks. You are going to be tied to a wild fish of *at least* 6 lb and, according to Laurence, it will fight like nothing else you have ever hooked before.

The fishery record for rainbow trout was broken in 1987 and now stands at 14 lb. The brown trout record is an incredible 11 lb 8 oz. Truly a magnificent fish. A point worth noting for those who prefer fishing for browns was given me by Laurence. Originally browns were found to be expensive to breed for fishing as they demanded a high food input for a slow growth rate. As well as being costly to feed on to a catchable size, they often skulked about the bottom feeding on snails and small fish, so missing the angler's flies in the surface layers. The Loch Leven strain of brown now being produced has proved to be a faster grower than the unusual cheetahs, tigers, and brook trout, so we may perhaps look forward to more fisheries stocking browns in the not too distant future.

SEASONAL TACTICS

In general, the same tackle can be used for any of the waters described in this book, but naturally there will be fly patterns and equipment that are local favourites.

Spring

With the cooler weather that spring often brings, the trout will be in competitive mood because of the lower water temperature and will move around more in search of food. Consequently, a floating line, coupled with a long leader, will produce the fish. I am a believer in using slow sinks early on, but at Furnace Brook the surface fishing will be most popular. Line sizes need be no more than No. 7 or 8, with corresponding rod sizes, as you will only need to cast 20 yards or so. Flies used at this time of year should be lures, or traditional favourites like the Vivas, Montana nymph, and Muddy Water. Retrieve speeds should be varied, but tends towards slow on a bright day, and faster on a cloudy or dark day.

Summer

There should be plenty of growth in the weedbeds by this time of year, with the north end of the lake producing Canadian Pondweed. Look for surface activity and use floating lines, or sink tips, with a slow retrieve. Start early, take it easy around high noon, and then fish hard again in the failing light. Drop your leader tippet down to 3 lb, but keep it about 10 ft long, and retrieve with big nymphs like the Mayfly, Walker's Nymph, or Green Beast. The topwater man should try Mayfly, Lacewing Olives, Sedge, Longhorn, or White Moth, and as there are plenty of alder trees surrounding the lakes, a Black Ant or Hawthorn fly could be useful. A local tip is the Cinnamon and Gold. Try looking for the deeper water with polarizing glasses and you may well see a rainbow closer to the bank than you would normally consider fishable.

Autumn

Although Daddy Longlegs do not really come into their own in this part of Sussex until the end of September, try them early anyway, just in case. Also good are the spinners, craneflies, and sedges, while the leaded flies also start to come in now. Where there is a fry population you can bet your fly wallet that the browns will be close by. Choose something like a Jersey Herd, Sinfoil's Special, or one of the Baby Dolls, but tied small. Cast alongside the margins as well as out in front of you. Remember that most of the fry will be hatched fingerlings, or smaller, of the native brown stock, so why not take a shot at tying up a pattern that resembles the colours of a brown trout fry?

Winter

Although the fishing is not so pleasant, the trout will still be there, although less enthusiastic about chasing the lures. Either that, or I'm just too cold to fish really hard! I confess to not being as enthusiastic myself in the depths of winter as I am in the summer. Vivas or any fry-shaped lure should produce, but don't bother with a fast strip. The colder water temperature will make the fish slower in responding to a passing lure, so give them time to take it, and be prepared for a casual pull, rather than the crash-take of the autumn fry feeders. One product worth using for nailing these nifty biters is the Airflo slow-sink line. With only a fractional amount of stretch in the fly line you will get an immediate response when a fish nips at the fly, and a sharp, gentle strike will set the hook. The fishery is also a lot quieter during the winter, so why not pick your weather patterns, and when you get a mild airflow moving across the country, that is the time to fish at Furnace Brook.

Even with a fringe of ice on the lake, Furnace Brook offers the chance of sport. Rainbows love cold water and a late-season session at this venue could put you in with the chance of some action.

GENERAL INFORMATION

As for angler facilities, Furnace Lake has a car park, a WC, and a fishing lodge. Other members of the family are welcome but, as Laurence states, 'must be on a lead!'. He has no objection to someone using the picnic facilities, but common sense should prevail, preventing beloved little Jimmy roaring round the margins in his pedal car to see what Dad has caught.

Fishing rules and times are fairly standard. No fly is allowed larger than a size 8 hook, although you can use dry fly, nymphs or lures. During summer the fishing will obviously get harder and dropping down to a 3 lb tippet is clearly better, provided you are careful with it and tie your knots correctly, than using one of 8 lb. There is no requirement to go down to a 1½ lb tippet, and anyone using such a fine leader with good fish is frowned upon. Starting times are around 8 AM and closing time is around one hour after sunset. This allows the angler to capitalize on that high-summer surface sport, when the last hour of light may be the only time that the trout are going to show.

There is the usual price structure for fishing. Day tickets are £15.00 for a four-fish limit; £8.50 two fish. There are discounts for bulk bookings, so if you have a group of friends in a small flyfishing club, or can get together a number of fishermen, take advantage of the saving. A season ticket is available, with a limit of two fish per visit. If you are a complete novice and have no tackle, Laurence will hire you some and may also put you in the better areas to boost your chances of getting a take. Rod-sharing is not allowed.

For more information contact: Laurence Ryan, Furnace Brook Trout Farm and Fishery, Trolliloes, Cowbeech, Nr Hailsham, East Sussex. Telephone: (0435) 830298.

LANGFORD FISHERIES

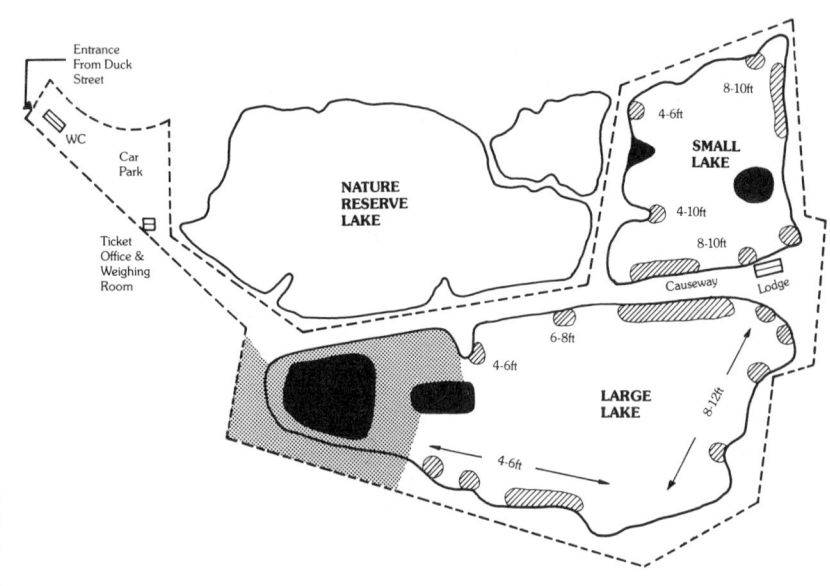

Entrance
From Duck
Street

WC

Car
Park

Ticket
Office &
Weighing
Room

**NATURE
RESERVE
LAKE**

4-6ft

8-10ft

**SMALL
LAKE**

4-10ft

8-10ft

Causeway

Lodge

6-8ft

4-6ft

**LARGE
LAKE**

8-12ft

4-6ft

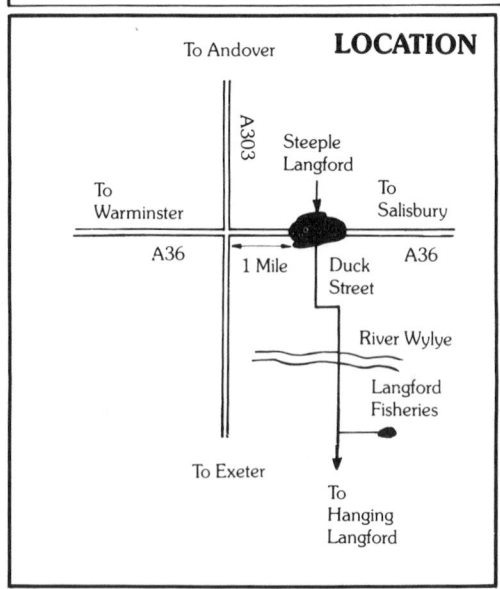

LOCATION

To Andover

A303

Steeple
Langford

To
Warminster

To
Salisbury

A36

1 Mile

Duck
Street

A36

River Wylye

Langford
Fisheries

To Exeter

To
Hanging
Langford

- - - - Site Boundary

Nature Reserve
Island or Point

Nature Reserve
(No Admittance)

 Hot Spots

Water Depths Shown in Feet

LANGFORD

The Wiltshire countryside is still one of the prettiest places to fish in our land, and Langford Fisheries lies in that county's Wylye valley, to the south of the Wylye, known to many for its secretive trout and grayling stocks. This is one of the more sheltered of the small trout waters, snugged down with hills to the north and south and water meadows to the east. There are three lakes in the area: two are the trout fishery, the third is a Nature Reserve, whose wildfowl and general bird life can be spectacular at times. Managed by Paul Knight, the site is based on worked out-gravel pits.

Fishing with rod and line first began at Langford in March 1984. At that time the larger lake was used purely for growing on fish, the vast majority of which were marketed through Billingsgate fish market. With attention focused on the table market, a sporting fishery was at that stage still very much a sideline, and it is only in recent years that the water has acquired its present status. The large lake was opened for fishing in June 1986, and although links with the commercial fishery are still provided by the floating trout pens, all stocks are now used for restocking the fishery. Because the fish farm is sited in the middle of the larger lake, a fair number of escapees have taken up residence over the initial three years and have actually grown on in the lake. This has produced a good head of semi-wild trout to spice up your sport.

On the opening day of the 1988 season a 12 lb rainbow was caught on this large lake, and in Paul's opinion this is still the best fish they have produced – certainly as far as quality is concerned – although not the largest. There is no comparison between the fight of a 12 lb semi-wild rainbow and that of a double-figure ex-brood model. Many of these trout resided under the trout cages, enjoying the easy life, and only nipping out when they felt the need for something extra. A lot have now been caught, or are indeed uncatchable, but enough remain under the cages, and these get caught from time to time, adding a bit of sparkle to a surprised fisherman's day.

The smaller lake has a wide range of depths from 2 ft to 10 ft by the steep causeway. The large lake ranges from 4 ft at the west end to 14 ft at the east end. I was amazed to hear from Paul that, as at many other waters, 1987 was his best-ever year. Some 5625 rods landed 16,300 fish in that year, which gives about the highest average I can find: 2.89 fish per rod. The record rainbow was also caught in 1987. Taken from the small lake, the fish weighed 17 lb. The brown trout record fell in the same season, when a fine fish of 6 lb 10 oz was landed from the large lake. During the last year alone, sixteen fish in double figures were caught, although Paul is quick to point out that Langford does not put itself forward as a big fish water. They aim for a 2 lb 4 oz average size, with the chance of a larger fish as a bonus.

APPROACH AND TACKLE

The two lakes are ideally suited to nymphing, with Canadian Pondweed being the dominant weed over the entire area during the summer. It rarely comes to the surface, except occasionally in the small lake. Green Tag stick flies, Montanas, Pheasant Tails, Damsel nymphs, and all colours of buzzer take fish. Dry flies are successful in their different seasons, and hawthorn, mayfly, and sedge are the most abundant natural flies. The usual lures take fish, with black or white being the most successful colours, although Paul limits hook size to a No. 10 long-shank hook in an effort to prevent anglers hurling budgie-style lures in the water.

A point worth noting here is that at Langford a team of flies is allowed. The method is strictly prohibited on many small waters because a fish that is broken off and trailing spare flies can be pursued by other trout trying vainly to snap up the flies. I have never heard of a team of lures being fished, but a team of buzzers fished in the surface film is a definite advantage, and so this unusual freedom should give you more confidence in using very small flies. On the subject of lost casts or leaders, Paul has a gripe about fishermen who leave nylon line lying around. I agree with him wholeheartedly, the

Langford Fisheries comprises two lakes. Long casting at the larger lake will often provide the chance of a good rainbow that may not have seen an angler's fly all day.

more so since a Nature Reserve backs on to the fishing lakes. We have had enough bad press from the anti-angling lobby, without giving them more ammunition. A lodge is due to be built soon, and Paul then hopes to educate people about the ways of water birds by mounting an exhibition explaining exactly what goes on in and around the lakes.

Regular visitors to Langford proved in 1987 that they can catch fish in all weathers with floating lines and small flies. Even in the coldest and roughest conditions, fish will feed in mid-water at some point during the day. Many of the regulars will fish with nothing but floating lines. It became very obvious that these year-round nymph anglers caught the better and longer-established fish. Although sunk lines and lures will always catch fish, Paul has seen a gradual change back to traditional wet flies, as well as to dry flies.

The manager of Langford, Paul Knight, shows off the quality of rainbow available at his fishery. In high summer, surface fishing can be particularly eventful for the angler wishing to stay on into the twilight hours.

In the autumn many fish were caught on floating line, a greased leader, and a white muddler fished across the surface – not true dry-fly style, but a step in the right direction as far as entertainment and excitement are concerned. Winter fishing has shown that the fish will still take small flies, but they must be fished very slowly, sometimes just letting the ripple do the work. The hawthorn is the first to hatch, around mid-April, and this then runs into a moderate mayfly hatch in late May and early June. Sedges appear from late spring, right through into the autumn, and autumn buzzer hatches can be very spectacular, especially, on the large lake.

Paul thinks that evening fishing with buzzers is the most popular of the natural techniques. During winter, provided the weather is not too cold, local hatches take place throughout the day and often bring fish close to the top, although these flies are 'smutty' and really too small to imitate. As for wind direction, the south-westerly air flows are more productive, but anything between south and north is good. An east wind can fish quite well here, once it has settled in, but a cold easterly can whip torturously down on the anglers as the fishery is located in an east–west valley. A settled wind is better to fish than one that cannot decide on one direction.

With surface nymphing being the most exciting technique, tackle can be kept slightly on the light side, even though there are some big fish at Langford. The ideal set-up is a 9–9½ ft rod, of a light but strong construction, such as an Orvis, coupled with a No. 6 line, weight-forward if required. Think of those semi-wild rainbows and you can see the need for a leader strength terminating in a breaking strain of at least 5 lb.

SEASONAL TACTICS

Spring

Try a slow-sink line with small lures, contrasting the colours rather than using multi-coloured types. A black or white Baby Doll should provide you with an idea of what they are hitting best. Alternatively you can stay on the surface with a dry fly, waiting for that hawthorn activity around mid-April. Try the deep end of the large lake early on in the morning, moving to the causeway and fishing the smaller lake by lunchtime. Then move around the small lake, trying the bays.

Summer

The fishing is much the same as in spring, except there is no need to get down at all. Everything should be fished on a floating line, a 10 ft leader and almost any nymph pattern you care to choose. In late June the Mayfly nymph will still work, as will Damsel and Montana. Try buzzers in teams through the surface film, with black or red predominant. Keep your retrieves slow, and be prepared for a crash take from one of those semi-wild fish. They will have seen all the larger flies, but often fall for a tasty morsel fished in the surface film.

Autumn

The main activity will still be on the floating lines, but I suggest trying the morning and midday periods with slow sinks, using traditional wet flies like Peter Ross, Butcher, or even a Teal Blue and Silver. The swing towards traditional wet flies is not merely fashionable – the fish take them as well! Try making your casts along the margins rather then straight out. Then fan-cast the area in front of you to search out any taking fish. It is certainly worth staying on until dark for a last-minute brown, and remember that they run to over 5 lb.

Winter

As previously mentioned, Paul's regulars have proved the fish still come out to floating lines and small flies. Lures will produce, but should be fished very slowly. Whiskey or any orange lure tied in miniature should catch. When the weather is variable it is always best to phone Paul first and see what his advice on fly choice and technique is.

GENERAL INFORMATION

Fishing at Langford is year-round, except for Christmas Day. It opens at 8.30 AM and you can fish through until dark. Half-day tickets finish or begin at 2.30 PM, although anyone arriving outside those hours is given a six-hour ticket. Evening tickets in summer begin at 5 PM. Once a limit is caught, fishing must stop until a further ticket is purchased. Rods and reels are on hire for £3.00 inclusive per session. Tuition will be available in late 1988 from qualified instructors, while the new lodge currently being built should be stocked with tackle, and a selection of flies from a professional source.

Prices at Langford are:

Day ticket: £17.00 (five fish limit).
Half-day ticket: £11.50 (three-fish limit).
Evening/Junior ticket: £8.00 (two-fish limit).

Pensioners may fish all day on a three-fish ticket if they wish. Rather than a season ticket, Paul offers a 50-fish ticket for £175. This enables the holder to fish as often as he likes to catch his trout, providing he still retains all the fish he lands. Langford is a popular fishery, and one of the best in this part of the Wiltshire countryside. For more information contact: Paul Knight, Langford Fisheries, Duck Street, Steeple Langford, Nr Salisbury, Wiltshire SP3 4NH. Telephone: (0722) 790770.

LEOMINSTEAD TROUT FISHERY

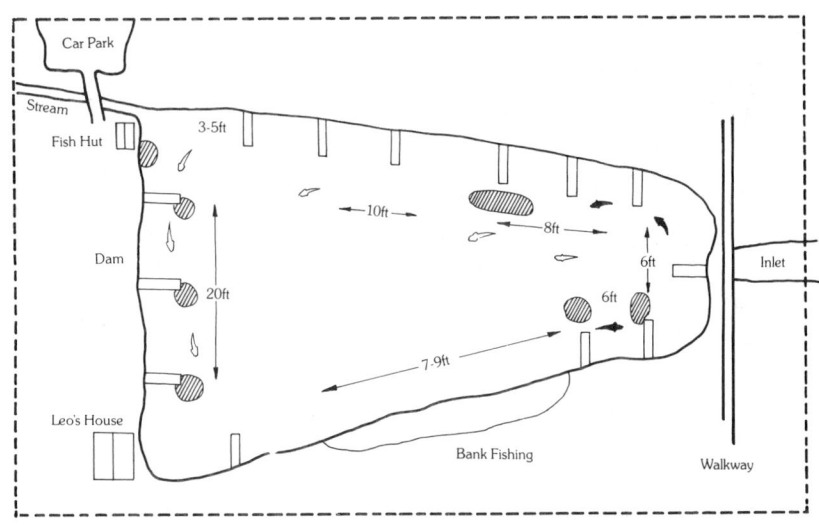

Car Park

Stream

Fish Hut

3-5ft

Dam

20ft

Leo's House

10ft

8ft

6ft

6ft

6ft

7-9ft

Bank Fishing

Inlet

Walkway

LOCATION

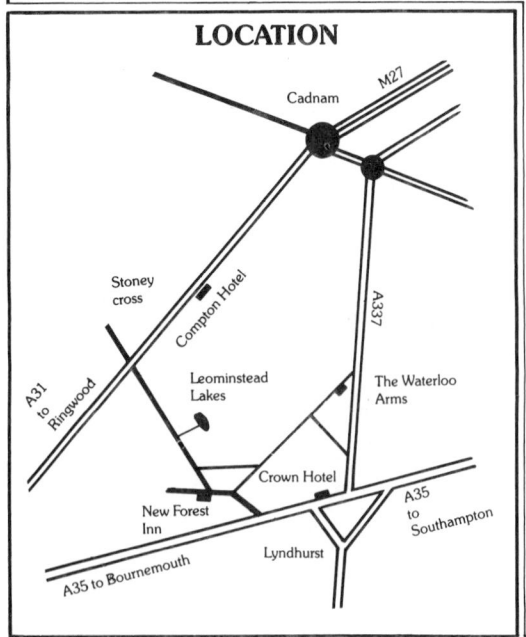

M27

Cadnam

Stoney cross

Compton Hotel

A337

A31 to Ringwood

Leominstead Lakes

The Waterloo Arms

Crown Hotel

New Forest Inn

Lyndhurst

A35 to Southampton

A35 to Bournemouth

Brown

Rainbow

Hot Spots

Water Depths Shown in Feet

LEOMINSTEAD

One of the strangest waters to fish in trout-rich Hampshire is Leominstead. I say strange, purely because you would think that the chalk hills percolating the spring water in this county would make every trout water gin-clear. Not so, Leominstead. Yet this fishery lies in one of the most picturesque settings imaginable. Situated in the heart of the New Forest, it is only five minutes from Junction 1 of the busy M27. Winding down a lane, you cross a cattle grid and are transported immediately into the peace and tranquillity of the forest. Wild ponies still graze freely on the surrounding grasslands, and early-morning fishermen may have the bonus of spotting some wild deer. It is difficult to believe just how close you are to busy main roads. Let us hope that the developers never get the chance to ruin one of the last unspoilt corners of southern England.

The market town of Lyndhurst is only ten minutes away, giving this fishery the ideal location, for the rest of the family can visit the town while the angler puts in a few hours of flyfishing. This water produces well throughout the summer and winter, the single lake providing consistent sport. It is stocked twice weekly with good-sized browns and rainbows up to nearly 15 lb, and also holds some natural wild browns. The lake was originally part of a large estate and was a coarse fishery before falling into disrepair. It was taken over many years ago by Leo Jarmal and his wife. After building its reputation as a quality big-fish venue, they left for Wales.

Many fishermen were sad to see one of trout fishing's characters move away, but the new owner, Gordon Strange, soon took over the task of maintaining Leominstead's reputation as a premier trout water. A trout fisherman himself, Gordon put all his efforts into maintaining the standard of fishing for his customers. The colour of the water is the key to its success. Fed by a stream entering through the forest, the brown peaty water at first looks unattractive. But put a fly through it a few times and you soon appreciate why so many anglers return here, including angling journalists and celebrities.

While many clear waters are good for stalking individual fish, this same clarity means that with too many anglers throwing fur and feather at a single fish, or a pricked trout, the fishing becomes difficult. Here, at Leominstead, the highly coloured water acts as a barrier that keeps the trout's association with trout anglers to a minimum.

The other advantage of this venue is the extensive treeline, which keeps even the strongest gale force wind at bay. You can throw a fly here when all the other fisheries have been blown off. Of course, these same trees and rhododendron bushes reach out and grab your back cast. I know, because I've left more than a few patterns up there myself. There can also be a lot of land-borne insects that find their way into the trout's diet, so that the feeding period lasts right through the day. While the water is over 10 ft deep at the base of the dam, most takes come about 2 ft down. This is strange, as you would usually think to pick up trout near the bottom, but for as long as I can remember, the surface to a depth of 2 ft was always the best area. Leo Jarmal always tried to drum it into me that I was fishing too deep, that it was far better to find the depth the trout cruise at than to worry about the pattern of fly. A weird approach, but one that seems to 'hold water'.

With Leominstead's coloured water comes a very high level of natural food, ensuring good winter fishing. The dark colour also shuts down the sunlight, so there is little in the way of snaggy weedbeds over much of the lake. I remember I was always sceptical about sea trout being able to find their way up the tiny stream and into the lake. Then one day Chris Dawn, at that time Features Editor of *Angling Times* and now editor of *Trout Fisherman*, stopped off at my house with a sea trout of about 3 lb. Since then I have realized there is always the outside chance of a bonus sea trout. All the stock fish put in are either females or triploids around 2 lb. The browns tend to be caught any time, but definitely start to show better towards the autumn. I often wonder, in the winter when the stream is running high, why the sea trout cannot be netted and placed in the stock pond for feeding on.

Make no mistake about the occupants of the dark peaty-coloured water of Leominstead . . . they can run big! This massive rainbow came from the right-hand edge of the garden bank, a recognized hotspot for bigger fish.

As the water is surrounded by both trees and rhododendron bushes right down to the edge, it has been necessary to build stages for the fishermen to cast from. A word of advice about these platforms: the trout don't always come at the extreme length of your cast, nor do you have to cast straight out in front of you. It is often better, especially if nobody is fishing from an adjacent platform, to make a sideways cast instead, as the browns tend to lurk near an empty stage. Be prepared for a big fish! The other point is that you can bring a fresh fish in too quickly. When this happens, remember that you are still in deep water and that 3 lb rainbow will dive under the staging supports with consummate ease.

If you hook one of the big rainbows from 7 lb up into double figures, the problem is even greater. Take your time playing the fish, and ease it in towards the staging only when you are confident it is either played out completely or that you can control those final surges. Use as big a landing net as you can, and make sure the fish goes in first time. Nothing wakes up a tired fish quicker than a blundering scoop with the landing net.

The fishery records for both species of trout are substantial, which is the main reason why the rules prohibit the use of leaders terminating in anything less than 5 lb breaking strain. The biggest rainbow ever caught there weighed 12 lb 13 oz, while the record brown trout was even bigger, at 13 lb 10 oz, which must make it one of the biggest browns ever taken on a fly in England. Leominstead is a Troutmaster venue and issues a much-coveted badge, signifying that the angler has landed a trout over 7 lb from the water.

The maximum depth at the base of the dam is thought to be 28 ft, but other than the odd hour scouring its depths with a fast-sink line, I suggest sticking to the top 2 ft of water. Most of the casting platforms are repaired each year, and there are now sixteen of them built out over the water, with another six stands of bank fishing called the garden area. This latter grassy bank is a good place to try for a big fish by working the right-hand edge where it drops away.

The 1986 catch statistics were good, with some very big fish taken. They break down as follows: 283 over 3 lb, 98 over 4 lb, 122 over 5 lb, 112 over 6 lb, 103 over 7 lb, 26 over 8 lb, 9 over 9 lb and 18 over 10 lb. The successful flies were Whiskey, Jack Frost, Jersey Herd,

When fishing from one of the stages, be careful of bringing the trout to net too quickly, as they can dive under the staging and cut the leader. A fate shared by many an enthusiastic angler at Leominstead!

Viva, Christmas Tree, and Baby Doll. Most patterns in the brighter colours will evoke some sort of response, so try anything that takes your fancy.

SEASONAL TACTICS

Spring

Try a slow-sink line in April and early May, as the water temperature may still be a bit cool. Although many trout will fall to surface fishermen, a deeper fly fished on a faster retrieve will cover more fish and put you in touch with bigger specimens. A 9 ft leader is adequate, but watch your back cast as it unrolls. The branches may not have many leaves yet, but they still catch the flies of the unwary caster! By mid-May and early June the water will have started to warm up a bit and the fish will show themselves nearer the surface. Change to a floating line, but keep to leaded nymph patterns so that the fly is still a foot or so deep. There should also be a bit of activity from the dry flies and land-borne insects. Check with Gordon which are the most successful patterns of the week. They should be Black Muddler, Whiskey fly, or any of the matukas. For deep lines fish a fast strip back, for 1–2 ft down make it slower, and don't lift off until you see that fly. Even then, pause a second in case there is a fish behind it.

Summer

As the water is sheltered, its temperature will rise fairly quickly. Thus the movement of the fish from a depth of 4 ft to an inch or so of the surface takes place over a few weeks. June and July will get more difficult because of the bright sunlight, so keep to small Pheasant Tail nymphs, corixas, and buzzers fished on a floating line. Make the retrieve slow, and always stay on until dusk. Spooky trout seldom rise during the brightest part of the day, and will feed right up until the last hour of fishing. They feed into darkness as well, but you won't be allowed to stay on that long. The dry flies may be difficult to imitate, yet several times I have seen anglers take a limit of rainbows, dragging a big Mayfly or Lee Wulff across the surface. The trout actually bow-waved after it, but I haven't had that same luck myself. Perhaps they take it for some sort of enormous pond skater!

Autumn

This is the time to search out the bush overhangs and free stages for the big brown trout that remain undaunted by the flies thrown at them. Why they feed better in autumn is puzzling, but many anglers think that the fish know the winter is coming and start to fatten up for the hard times. I think it is more likely to be that any fry eggs will have hatched into tiny fish and thereby become a main part of the brown trout's diet. While rainbows cruise around looking for food, the brownie will lie near an overhang, zipping out to snaffle a small fry when it gets the chance. Accurate casting with patterns like Whiskey fly, Gold Muddler, or the traditional Jersey Herd should put you in touch. Stay with floating lines, on ripply days, going to an Airflo slow-sink on still days. Try to cover as many fishing platforms as you can, and remember that the rainbows will fall to this method of careful casting just as much as the big browns.

Winter

Not my favourite time of year for fishing any water, but this fishery should still see some of its occupants coming out. With the drop in the water temperature will come the need to get your fly down near the bottom. If you fish the dam area you have depths to 20 ft and that calls for an Airflo fast-sink line. Grease your leader and use a buoyant pattern like the muddlers, allowing the fly to be above the dead leaves on the bottom. You should fish as slowly as you can, with just a few jerks during each cast to spark up any trout following the fly closely but not taking. Try some of the Baby Doll colours like yellow,

A regular at Leominstead is Desirree Strange, who often outfishes the men. Here she brings a rainbow to net from the staging platform.

red, or lime green at the opposite end of the fishery where the shallow water will warm slightly during a wet south-westerly airflow. Stay in the area if you get a few plucks, varying your pattern and retrieve until you hit a fish.

GENERAL INFORMATION

The venue is open all year, with fishing times from 9 AM to 9 PM or sunset, whichever is the earlier. A half-day ticket covers from 3 PM to 9PM or sunset, and is variable from September as the days get shorter. The bag limit of trout is four fish for a full-day ticket, and two fish for a half-day ticket. Rod-sharing is strictly forbidden. All fish caught should be recorded in the fishery book to ensure correct restocking. Permitted methods are dry and wet-fly fishing only. The maximum hook size is 10, the maximum length of lures is 1 in overall, and no tandems, droppers, or barbless hooks are allowed. Only single hooks must be used, with a cast strength of not less than 5 lb. All fisherman must have a landing net of not less than 20 in in width, plus a priest for despatching the fish. It is forbidden to return fish to the water, and all trout over 9 in must be killed. Once the bag limit is reached, the fisherman must stop fishing. If a second ticket is purchased, the angler must change position to the opposite bank. Fishermen must not take over another's place, nor leave tackle where they are not fishing. No dogs or children are allowed. In bad winter conditions the charge is based on the poundage of fish caught. Advance booking is advisable, particularly for weekends and bank holidays. Club days and private block bookings are welcome mid-week. A hot meal can be provided in the lodge if booked in advance. Fishing weekends, whole weeks can be arranged with the cooperation of the local hotels.

Ticket prices are as follows:

Day ticket: £15.00 (four-fish limit).
Half-day ticket: £9.00 (two-fish limit).

For more information contact: Gordon Strange, Leominstead Trout Fishery, Emery Down, Lyndhurst, Hampshire SO4 7GA. Telephone: (042128) 2610.

Des Strange with a super Leominstead rainbow of 6 lb.

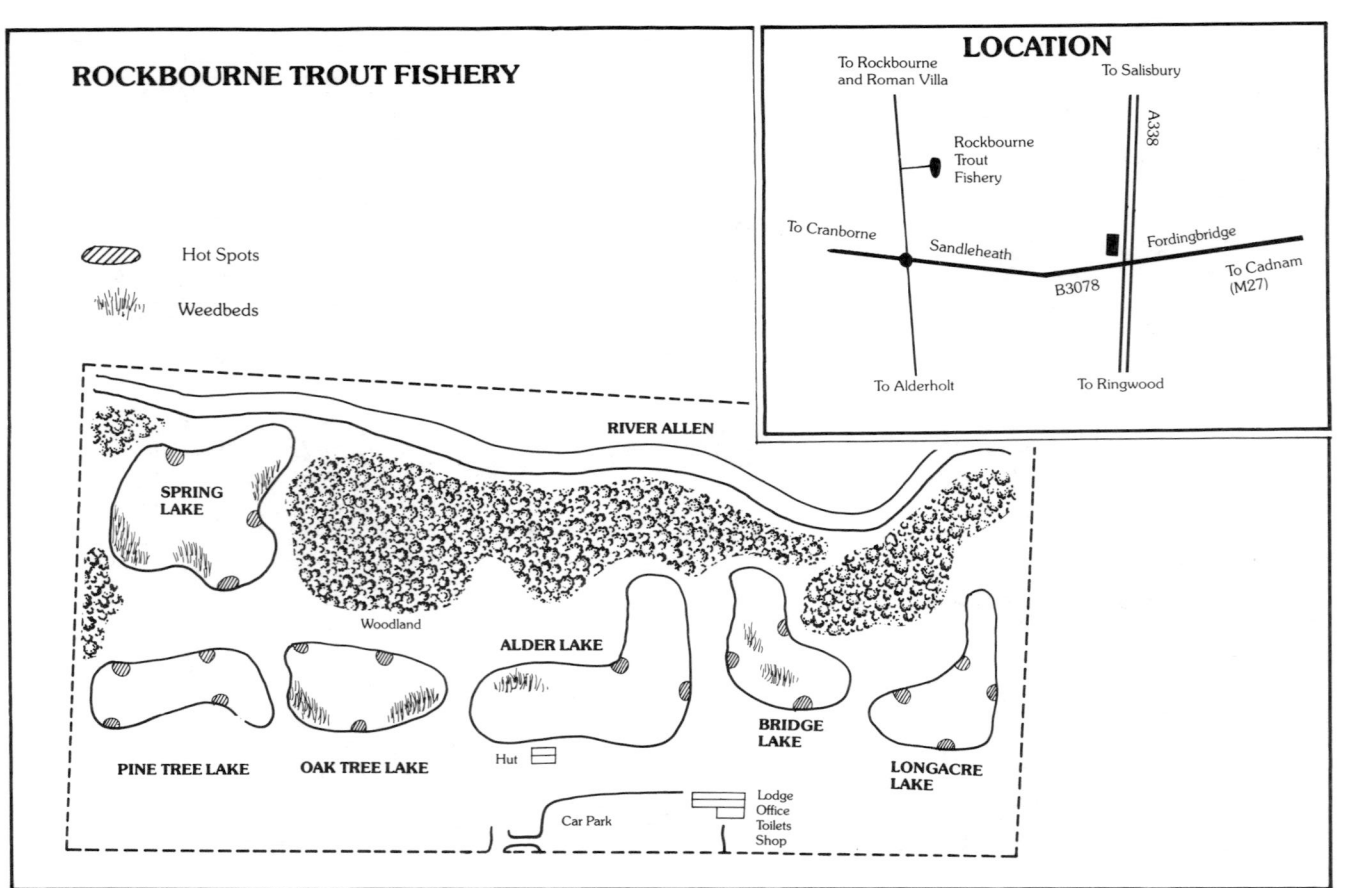

ROCKBOURNE TROUT FISHERY

Hot Spots

Weedbeds

LOCATION

To Rockbourne
and Roman Villa

To Salisbury

A338

Rockbourne
Trout
Fishery

To Cranborne

Sandleheath

Fordingbridge

To Cadnam
(M27)

B3078

To Alderholt

To Ringwood

RIVER ALLEN

SPRING
LAKE

Woodland

ALDER LAKE

BRIDGE
LAKE

LONGACRE
LAKE

PINE TREE LAKE

OAK TREE LAKE

Hut

Car Park

Lodge
Office
Toilets
Shop

ROCKBOURNE

Hampshire certainly has more than its fair share of quality small water trout fisheries. The western corner of the county is fringed by the New Forest, and the water meadows of the Avon valley provide the watershed for the foundation of any lakes. Although the Hampshire Avon is not the river it was, it still provides the quality and clarity that create near-perfect conditions for trout waters. However, it should be noted that one theory on the decline of the Hampshire Avon is that the overabundant trout farms create an effluent of their own that stifles the chances of any coarse fish fry in the areas downstream. Current research into this decline will doubtless reveal more than one factor in the demise of the river but, even so, it is still one of the better coarse fishing rivers in the south of England.

In the area around Fordingbridge there are several excellent small trout waters, possibly the most productive being Rockbourne, at Sandleheath, on the outskirts of Fordingbridge. There are presently some six lakes open for sport, plus a section of the tiny River Allen. The fishery was first formed in the early 1970s with the digging of Longacre lake at the far eastern end of the property. Over the years, other small lakes were dug and the present six together form one of the most productive waters I have ever experienced. The water table lies only a few inches below the ground level, which made it necessary to excavate the lakes quickly, as they also filled with water faster than other areas. The faster a lake fills, the easier it is for weeds and insects to establish themselves, thereby creating a ready source of nourishment for any trout.

The actual sub-stratum of the property is a mixture of clay and gravel, boosted by a good flow of underground spring water to each lake. The water has settled into a gin-like clarity as quickly as the second year after excavation. The property lies in a gently falling gradient on the old floodplain of the Hampshire Avon valley, and comes under the classification of a wetland with its surrounding alder and willow trees. There is consequently a natural haven for any land-borne insects, which inevitably find their way onto the water, and into the trout's diet.

The first stocking of trout was in 1970 and the new owner-managers Tony Hern and John Cain now stock on a daily basis, so that there are always plenty of trout going in to the various lakes. They have their own stock ponds where the fish are fed on from fry until they reach the required size, and are then moved just a few hundred yards into their respective lakes. A small board by each lake gives the rod limit for that water, to prevent overcrowding. If the rod limit has been reached on a particular lake, simply move on to another. This is a good idea as it avoids undue pressure on any individual lake, all being quite small.

Many fisheries are open all year round, but as the traditional season runs from around mid-March to the end of October, I shall confine the fishery statistics to that period. To gain an idea of the popularity this water enjoys – and remember popularity must be borne out of trout being caught – digest the ofllowing. In 1987, a staggering 3703 rods caught 9631 trout, which averages 2.6 fish per rod and the average weight was 3 lb, which is quite incredible. Since Tony has taken over Rockbourne it has gained respect from many anglers because it has a reputation for giving a fair deal. As if 3 lb for an average were not enough, in the same year there were 834 trout over 4 lb caught. Attendance was even up by 11 per cent on the 1986 figures, and I would say that this fishery, under the existing management, is the best water in terms of value for money in the south of England. The fishery record for rainbow is 14 lb 4 oz, and was set in 1988. The fishery record for brown trout, 10 lb 7 oz, was also set in 1988.

Although Rockbourne is sheltered by the surrounding woodland, wind direction does have a bearing on catches. As usual, an easterly effectively kills off any hope of surface fishing with the dry fly, and it is the warm south-westerlies that bring the fish on. I sometimes wonder if so many anglers fish in the lethargic manner on an easterly that the trout don't come out because of the anglers' apathy. Mind you, I

Another river brownie for Adrian Hutchins, fishing one of the stream beats at Rockbourne.

have fished hard in easterlies and had only meagre results.

Start-of-season dates for trout are constantly changing, but Rockbourne is open from around mid-March until the end of October. After this, the winter fishing continues through until New Year's Day. Fishery rules are fairly standard, with a maximum hook size of No. 8, and no droppers allowed. A single fly is permitted, which can be one too many when you get caught up in the trees and bushes! If you are a novice there is tackle for hire at a nominal charge of £3.00 for a set and qualified instruction is available for those wishing to brush up on their techniques. The instructor has a Grade 1 NAC certificate and lessons, which must be booked, cost £10.00 per hour. The NAC qualification also incorporates fly tying, so there is nothing to stop you inventing a fly pattern, tying it with the instructor, then going out and catching a trout on it. A new tackle shop and fishery office selling a full range of flyfishing tackle and also some fly dressing materials is now open.

Not only does this fishery offer the six lakes but it has several beats on Sweatford's Water, which I always call the River Allen. This is a stream that joins the Hampshire Avon as a tributary two miles downstream from Fordingbridge. It supports a population of native brown trout and is also stocked with rainbows. Here is some really interesting sport, as you can book a beat for an extra £3.00, which allows you to fish the lakes until you get fed up and then move to the river in the knowledge that nobody has been on that beat to disturb the fish.

The last time I fished the stream I was amazed at the number of rainbows hiding under the streamer weed, and getting them out was far more interesting than fishing the lakes. I ended up taking my biggest river rainbow on upstream nymphing. I returned the fish, which was about 5 lb, to provide sport for another day. Any fish caught can either be retained as part of your limit, or released. The stream has a reputation for giving up its occupants in late morning, or again in the evening. The recommended methods are dry fly or upstream nymph.

Pine Tree lake holds the deepest water, with areas at each end falling to almost 20 ft, which is where many of the largest trout are taken. It is a lake most noted for its hatches of pond olives and buzzer. Spring lake is the clearest and most prolific of the group. It has a tremendous damselfly and dragonfly hatch, together with good numbers of pond olive, sedge and buzzer. Perhaps the most scenic lake, Pine Tree is extremely well sheltered and worth a few throws in the rough weather. I once took an 8 lb rainbow from this lake that appeared out of nowhere, even though the water was clear.

Oak Tree lake has vastly differing depths, with a good holding area

For a few pounds you can reserve a length of river to yourself, fishing it any time of the day. That way you get the best of the lakes early on, and can then take things easier in the afternoon. Here the author holds a rainbow from a stream beat. Rockbourne is one of the best fisheries in the south for a beginner to visit, as it enjoys a very high catch return.

around the edge of the weedbeds on the southern bank. Very good for surface fishing, it is possibly the best lake for dry fly, with olives, sedge, buzzer and damselfly all prolific. Alder lake is the newest of the six, and has established itself as a classic nymphing water, but also boasts a good hatch of mayfly. The smallest water is Bridge lake, which is good for damselfly, sedge and mayfly. Longacre Lake, supplemented by the stream, is a great water for the sedge, but also for corixa, shrimp and mayfly.

SEASONAL TACTICS

Spring

The water should be heaving with hungry trout, and on such small lakes the rod and line weights can be kept down to maximize sport. Carbon-fibre rods with an AFTM (Association of Fishing Tackle Manufacturers) rating of 5–7 are quite sufficient, and a double-taper line allows a quiet presentation. There is no need to crash a shooting head into the far bank! Leader length is important in this clear water, and local wisdom recommends a leader of up to 20 ft, for surface nymphing. A slow-sink line or an intermediate with a standard 9 ft leader is the norm for larger nymphs.

This tackle can be used throughout the entire season. Start with the slow sink, using short jerks to retrieve patterns like Mini Dolls, Whiskey fly, or Viva lure. The colour bias is towards orange or white. Even in spring you should be able to spot individual fish, but when using the long leader wait until you can actually see the fly before you lift off for the next cast. In the early season, big trout of over 4 lb will often follow a fly right to the bank before taking.

Summer

This is a prime time for visual stalking, floating lines, and either dry fly or leaded nymphs. There is no need to go to a sinking line, and my own preference is for short casts to a stalked fish. You simply lead the fish with a leaded nymph six feet in front of it and then take the nymph off its nose. You strike when you see that big white mouth open and close. Quite the most exciting and satisfying method of

Adrian Hutchins on another stream beat.

summer nymphing! The best patterns to try are Montana Nymph, Mayfly, Pheasant Tail, and Damsel Nymph. Summer is a good time of year to try the dry fly on the rainbows and browns in the stream beats, but take care, for they see you long before you can see them!

For dry fly stick to Olives and Mayfly, and make sure you hang on until the last hour. Even if a lake has received a lot of attention all day, you'll be suprised at how many fish will show in the falling light conditions.

Autumn

Stick to the leaded nymphs, but this time use an intermediate or slow-sink line. Retrieve in sharp jerks, alternating with slow pulls. The jerking action simulates a struggling nymph, and the slow motion is when you are most likely to get a take. The Daddy Longlegs will give good surface sport in the September evenings, and the Cinnamon and Sedge also serve well. Try a few lures in early October, but keep them small and you won't spook too many fish. Small Mini Dolls and the Appetiser tied on smaller hooks than you buy in the tackle shops work well. Check with the fly-tying instructor and see if you can devise a new pattern, since virtually any lure will work if fished correctly.

Make sure, if you continue stalking, to take a careful peek around the margins of the deeper pools. If a lake has been rested for even half an hour, the big fish will rest up quietly near the edges of weedbeds or drop-offs. A good presentation, almost the length of the leader, can generally get a response, and this is the way most big trout enthusiasts work. Spot the fish before somebody else does and blip a weighted nymph in front of its nose.

GENERAL INFORMATION

Opening time is 8.30 AM and closing time is half an hour after sunset. The half-day division is at 2 PM, and junior rod tickets are for those under the age of 16. Evening tickets begin at 4.30 PM, and Clubs or Associations may book the fishery for the entire day by prior arrangement. Wessex Water Authority rod licences are available from the fishery office. Ticket prices are subject to change each year, but the current prices are as follows. A day ticket, which gives a five-fish limit as opposed to the usual four fish, is £18.00. A half-day ticket gives a four-fish limit for £15.00, and the evening ticket gives three fish for £12.00. Blocks of tickets will be discounted, a scheme which is well worth taking advantage of because you only have to get 5 visits to get a 5 per cent discount, whilst 10 visits attract a $7\frac{1}{2}$ per cent discount. That's worth thinking about, especially if you get to like the sport there! The management can also organize accommodation to suit all tastes, at the Ashburn Hotel in Fordingbridge, the Compasses Inn at Damerham, or the Victoria Guesthouse at Sandleheath.

The aim of the fishery management is to provide high-class trout fishing in an atmosphere of relaxation and seclusion. I think Rockbourne has achieved that and can do no more than recommend a visit. Further details are available from: John Cain, Rockbourne Trout Fishery, Rockbourne Road, Sandleheath, Nr Fordingbridge, Hampshire SP6 1QG. Telephone: (07253) 603.

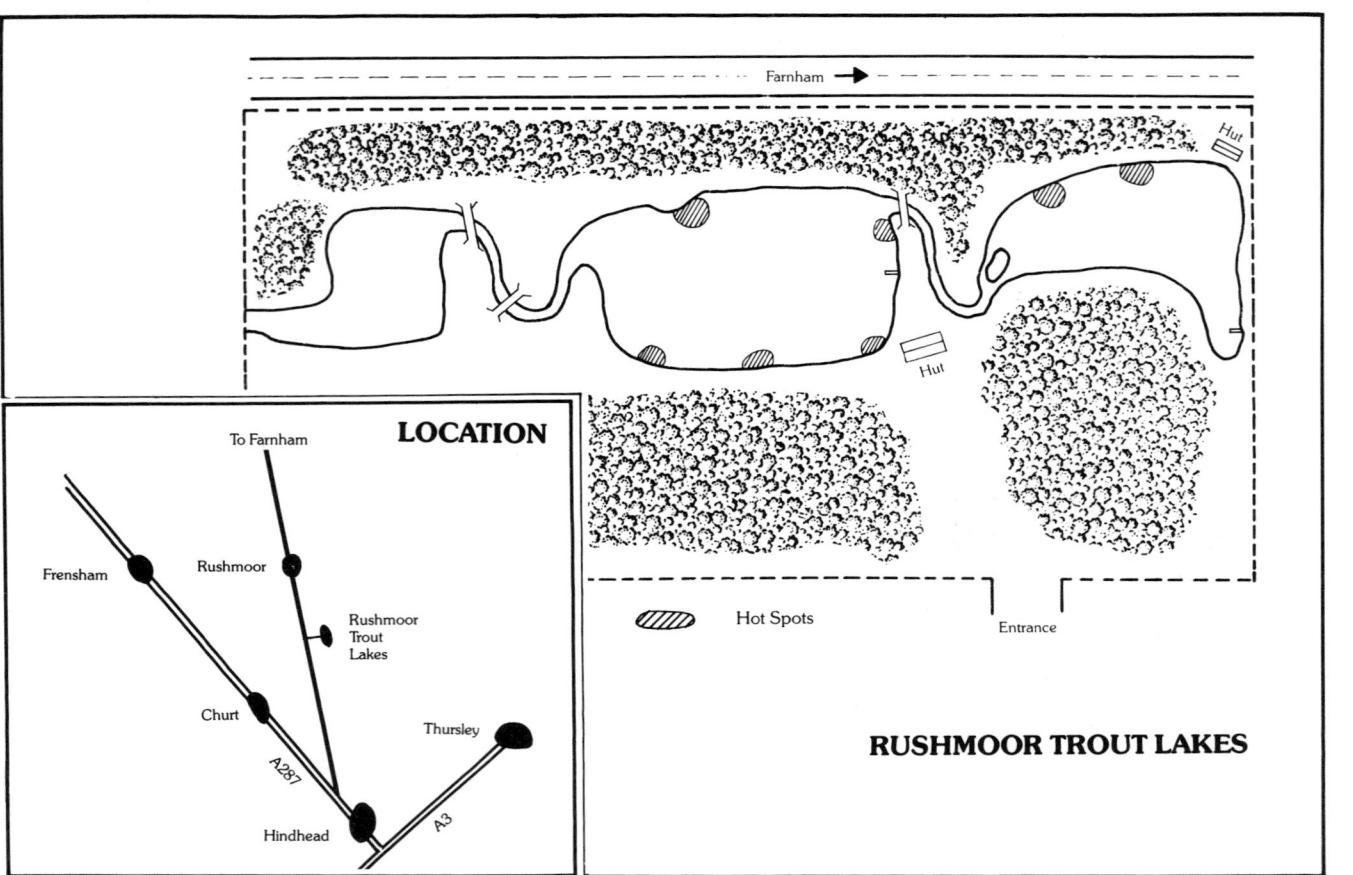

Farnham →

Hut

Hut

Hot Spots

Entrance

RUSHMOOR TROUT LAKES

LOCATION

To Farnham

Frensham

Rushmoor

Rushmoor
Trout
Lakes

Churt

Thursley

A287

Hindhead

A3

RUSHMOOR

Nowadays, small water trout lakes are a well established feature of the flyfishing scene. Yet only about fifteen years ago there was a hue and cry over offering trout fishing on a day-ticket basis, for the trend was regarded as prostituting the sport of the aristocracy. Thankfully, the small waters have survived the fusillade of words and have given the ordinary angler the key to unlock the door to the rainbow. I have approached this chapter a little differently as I would like the visitor to Rushmoor to use his own judgement in finding the best way to extract trout from this tiny fishery.

When the first day tickets started, the list of venues was fairly limited. But after a few years others started to open up, introducing competition into this line of business. To win customers you need an angle. With fishermen, providing the lure of outsize fish was the obvious approach. Rightly or wrongly, this system is still with us, but fortunately some fisheries have reverted to providing the discerning angler with attractive, well kept surroundings as well as maintaining a stocking policy that provides quality fish.

While travelling in the south of England, where the birth of small waters took place, I came across a little known fishery called Rushmoor Trout Lakes. To fish here, especially mid-week when it is less busy, is to savour the delights of solitude. The three small, secluded lakes are situated in a pleasant wooded valley near Hindhead in Surrey. A stream feeding them rises about a mile away and the flow varies little even in the driest weather. Apart from when there are flash floods, which will colour any water, the clarity is excellent, especially in the two main lakes. The fishery is run by Mr. D. Whitehead and the tickets are issued in advance.

The lakes were cleared just over ten years ago, the first major jobs being dredging and reclamation, which took some two years to complete. 'Monks' were then put in. These are a system to let water through each lake without pressuring the dam. Backing on to MOD land, the lakes had been virtually unused since the Second World War. Now, by dint of hard work, they have been transformed into a prolific fishery. Both lakes are stocked substantially before the season starts and are then topped up every month, depending on the number of fish taken. For such a small fishery with a monthly stocking policy there has to be a catch. There is, but it is in the angler's favour. This was one of the first waters to adopt the principle of catch and return, which ensures a stock of fish that after being caught and returned, can provide the angler with an interesting challenge. After the bag limit of four fish has been reached, instead of packing up the angler can fish on, catching as many trout as he wants. But he must use a barbless fly, so that they can be returned unharmed. Stocking is mostly with rainbows from 1 lb up to 5 lb, and with a few browns up to 4 lb.

APPROACH AND TACKLE

The fishery record is just on 10 lb, but the best sport is had by trying for the ½ lb fish using with tackle and small hooks. Lures are banned, as are hooks larger than size 10 long shank. When I visited the water with Essex angler Jerry Airey, we found plenty of taking fish about 3 ft deep, yet many took a miniature lime-green Baby Doll fly inched slowly across the bottom. There is an abundance of freshwater snails and shrimps, which I assumed to be the reason for taking the fish low in the water. The lakes are basically clay bottomed, with depths varying from shallows to deep holes of 8–10 ft. The surrounding woodland provides plenty of terrestrial insects, while the end of spring sees a terrific mayfly hatch. Buzzer hatches are common and can occur at any time throughout the day because of the sheltered position of the lakes.

I found an interesting way to take fish was to walk the margins slowly with a tiny brook rod. Providing nobody has been stamping around for at least an hour, it really is amazing the number of rainbows you can see just lying 'on station', or patrolling slowly up and down. A word of caution here. If you should spot such a fish, try

A light brook rod, a light leader, and a small nymph will give you good sport at Rushmoor Trout Lakes, and the fishery has a strict limitation on rod numbers, so overcrowding is no problem.

to throw well past him and parallel to the bank, not straight out. Many of the margin insects venture only a small distance from the sanctuary of bankside weeds. The trout know this and will take your fly confidently very close to the bank. In fact I always make a point of looking down the leader as I prepare to lift off for another cast. You'll be surprised how often you see the head and shoulders of a rainbow behind the fly. All the regular patterns will catch: green, red, or brown nymphs, Damsels, Pheasant Tails, and even the traditional wets like Butcher and Zulu.

GENERAL INFORMATION

Rushmoor is open from 1 April until the end of October. A day permit allows a four-fish limit (£17.00); half day (£9.00) two fish. After reaching the limit, just relax, tie on a barbless fly and see how many more you can take. Jerry and I took around twenty fish on this catch-and-return basis, thoroughly enjoying ourselves in the process. If you have a small club then Mr Whitehead can give a discount for a bulk booking, but remember to keep the numbers down. That way you can look into every bay and weed patch for that individual fish. Situated only some ten minutes from Hindhead on the Tilford and Farnham road, Rushmoor Trout Lakes make a pleasant change from the hustle and bustle of the big fish scene. For more information contact: D. Whitehead, Rushmoor Trout Lakes, Random Beach Road, Haslemere, Surrey. Telephone: (0428) 2818.

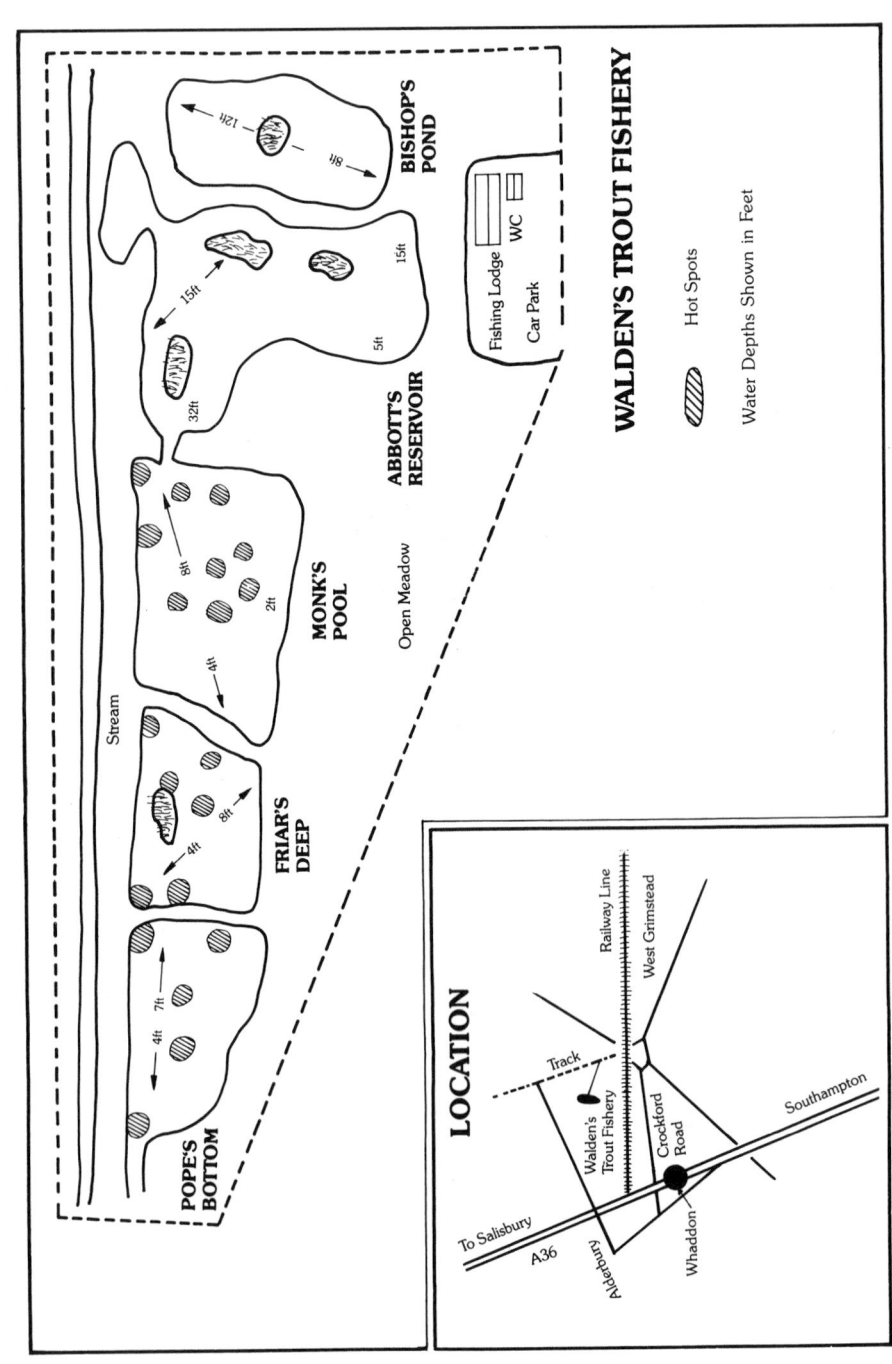

WALDEN'S TROUT FISHERY

WALDEN'S

I found no difficulty at all in adhering to the rules laid down by owner Mark Dawson for fishing at Walden's. Catch and release was the order of the day, and I think that this arrangement is the most appropriate for modern small water trout fishing. All small waters need stocking heavily with large 'battery' fish in order to compete favourably with the larger venues, but I think many writers deceive themselves when they try to create a mystery around catching these fish.

Having spent two or three years being fed on pellets, three or four times a day, the fish are then tipped into a lake. Allowing for a few hours to adjust, they are soon swimming around looking for someone to feed them. Far from their being wary of anglers, I have actually experienced them swimming towards me in the hope that I would start throwing the pellets in. What do you do? Crouch and carefully present a beautifully tied fly to what you think is a wary trout? Rubbish! If that fish has been recently stocked and you are the first angler down to the water, you will catch that fish, probably on the first cast, but please don't claim a large degree of skill for such an exercise.

If you release that fish after the struggle and let him swim free, it may be the next day that he sucks another fly in. Release him again, and it will be several days, maybe a week, before he looks at the fly again. After a month of being caught and returned his natural defences are honed a little more, so that you will have to think up ways of enticing him. Only then can you honestly say you deserved that fish.

You may think I am talking a load of old claptrap. Well, I have held this theory for years, in complete contrast to the dyed-in-the-wool trout men who thought the earth would stop turning if you ever released a trout. I've seen people so irate with me returning a trout alive that I'm surprised they don't walk round the lake with a sandwich board saying 'The end is nigh . . . don't release trout!' However, my theory, and that of others of course, has been proved right, and it is Walden's fishery in Wiltshire that is doing the proving. Mark Dawson was one of the first to try catch-and-release, yet even he was amazed at how much his anglers enjoyed not having the pressure of catching their 'limit' of trout.

Mark's stocking policy favours fighting triploid rainbows from 3 lb up to about 12 lb, which, having been hooked before, go off like an express train. Of course you have to get them to take your fly in the first place, but as the water is gin-clear you have the excitement of seeing them react to different patterns and retrieves. Walden's is modern as far as this policy goes, but I feel sure others will follow suit when they realize its popularity.

Personally, I find it all a hassle having to lug your catch around all day, and then gut them, bag them, freeze them, and so on. I would just as soon put the fish back, because I know they will create a much better adversary when I meet them the next time around. Whereas you always go crazy to get your limit where that system is in force, a catch-and-release policy allows a more leisurely approach. You can fish right through the day, and of course the more trout you catch, the more you can afford to experiment with new flies and techniques. You tend not to do that at other fisheries, when you only have four fish to go for.

The three established lakes are Pope's, Friar's and Monk's, which were converted around 1969 from a monks' stew pond. The water was at that time stocked with brown trout and run as a limited syndicate until Mark bought the lakes in 1984. He carried out extensive improvements, deepening Pope's and Friar's and, above all, improving the water flow. He stocked with rainbows and browns and opened as a put-and-take fishery in March 1986. Even though in the first year of fishing a lot of trout were taken, Mark soon became disillusioned with put-and-take fisheries, and realized that not all the anglers wanted to kill the fish. On many trips to America I have noticed that it is frowned upon to kill trout, many streams operating a no-kill policy. It is we here in Britain who are dragging our feet in bringing in new policies to suit the modern angler.

The author shows a prime condition 7 lb rainbow that fought hard. This one was taken out for the photograph with the owner's permission, but normally fish must be unhooked in the water.

Walden's has the added bonus of being set in beautiful surroundings, with natural flowering meadows and the backdrop of a pine forest. The lake bed is made of clay and the water feed comes mainly from a series of springs. Although gin-clear in the summer, the water does have a tendency to colour up during the winter.

Such has been the success of this new venture that Mark has had two more small lakes excavated during 1987 which he hopes to open in the 1988 season. That will give a total water area of five lakes and 7¼ acres, and there is the tiny stream of the Dun, which is a minor tributary of the Test, running along the edge of the forest. Three hundred years ago the entire area was under water, in the form of a reservoir to feed the Salisbury to Southampton area. Since the lakes are spring fed, there is a slight flow that prevents minor freezing, so always phone if you fancy a winter session, as the chances are quite good that they will be fishable.

It is nice to learn that the owner is no slouch with a fly rod either. I believe he holds the fishery record for trout caught and released with a total of over thirty fish. I once had a catch of 23 fish, including two seven-pounders for a total weight of 100 lb, so I know how difficult it is to take thirty-plus. Doubtless his expertise owes something to the fact that he used to fish bass commercially from Poole harbour using live sandeels. His best joint catch weighed in the region of 350 lb. The two new lakes will also incorporate some form of catch and release, and Mark hopes to move the fishery lodge into a larger building and to provide a range of hot food and drinks. Limited cooked meals, including early breakfast, are available at the moment.

The natural fly hatches can be especially good on Monk's pool, which hosts an exceptional hatch of olives. There are good hatches of sedge throughout the summer, plus the usual buzzers, damsels, and the like. There is a very sparse hatch of mayfly. Wind is never really a problem as the lakes have a massive protective screen of forestry, as well as being set in a slight valley. You can catch fish at any time throughout the year providing there is not a coating of ice on the water.

SEASONAL TACTICS

Spring

As the fishery is open all year round, there is not a mad rush of early-season takers, and the fish will have seen at least some anglers throughout the winter months. Even though the lakes, especially Monk's, are relatively shallow, I would advise an Airflo No. 7 forward-taper intermediate or slow sinker, with a rod to match, thus keeping the fly about 2 ft below the surface. Flies can be anything you wish as there is no restriction on sensible patterns, so try a leaded jig with a marabou tail, whipping it back in fast jerks. The takes will stop you solid.

The water should also be clear in Pope's and Friar's so take a careful look round in the deeper pools to see what is moving. With an intermediate line you can get down that extra foot to put the fly in front of them. For the shallow weeded area in the centre of the main lake, fire out and pop the fly through the weed. Of course you'll get

In clear water summer conditions, the angler will do well to check out the margins for cruising big fish, for they can often be fooled into taking the fly only a leader's length out.

weed staying on the hook from time to time, but you'll also get the odd fish hanging on too. Late spring is the time to start thinking of nymphs proper, and for early March and April I would advise sticking to lures.

Summer

This is the best time to visit Walden's, particularly to test your eyes and arm with a bit of visual stalking. Many of the trout will be around the margins of all of the lakes, and a clumsy cast will send them bow-waving into the centre. It is more important to present the fly in direct opposition to the trout's direction. This is because you don't want the fish to see the leader, and a better response is always obtained in this manner. Change to No. 6 floating fly lines, which are quite sufficient as most of the fish will be with 15 yards, many just a roll cast away.

In bright summer conditions the fish will show best in the early morning and late evening, epecially the latter, when the dry fly enthusiast will actually outfish the nymph man. Although there is a minimal mayfly hatch, a dry mayfly scores well in those failing hours of light, as does a white moth. Around midday, especially when it is hot, you will see the trout rising madly out in the centre of the main lake, taking insects that come off the shallow weedbed. Don't lay back in the sunshine. Throw out a long line with your choice of dry fly on and leave it as long as possible. You really have to keep concentrating, because if you look away then back to your fly, you forget where it was and miss the rise!

Autumn

While anglers at many slightly larger stillwaters will be moving on to the lures of fry feeders, the trout at Walden's will be even more perceptive about what is in front of them. They will have been caught and returned many times so rather than grading up to bigger lures for autumn, you should drop *down* to tiny weighted nymphs such as Pheasant Tails and the like. Takes must be almost entirely visual, so you need to watch the trout's mouth to see when it opens and closes as it takes the tiny nymph. The strike should be an instantaneous flick of the wrist, not too strong as you will be hitting the fish at close range.

Just enough to set the hook.

Although the standard larger weighted nymphs like Montana, Mayfly, Green Beast, and so on, come invariably on a size 8 hook, why not tie your own up on smaller hooks like size 12s? The tying is exactly the same, but the fish will be far more responsive to these smaller nymphs. Another tip is to fish a floating line, sunk leader, and muddler in the last hour of light on Monk's lake. Shoot out into the shallow weeded centre and strip back fast. Takes will be spectacular to say the least, and any trout hooked will melt line from your reel as it has nowhere else to go in such shallow water. This is one of the best times of year at Walden's, but remember late September will see the sun moving round the sky in a lower arc, so that you will spot the fish closer in.

Winter

Now is the time to go over to lures. Local favourites are Viva, Baby Doll, and Appetiser. Fish them on a floater or intermediate quite slowly, and lift into any pecking feeling you get when you retrieve. Takes will be similar to when you pull into a weedbed, or the fly pecks a piece of twig on the bottom. These trout are cagey and need to be fished for with skill.

I hear that Mark has introduced another method that I have always said we should progress to: night fishing for trout. With small cyalume lightsticks now available in a size suitable for tying into a lure, I think we may see more of this done. After all we fish for sea trout at night, so why not rainbows? Walden's has a floodlight rigged up on Monk's pool and early experiments have proved successful. For this reason fishing has been extended to 9 PM, and I recommend giving it a try, so that you can form your own opinion as to whether it is a new branch of flyfishing.

GENERAL INFORMATION

Instruction, should you be a complete novice, is available by advance booking and cost £15.00 per hour, plus the cost of fishing. Like many fisheries, I would suggest you defray this cost among two or three of you, as the same methods can be learned by all. Now for some of the rules. This is a big fish water, so do not drop much below a 6 lb leader tippet. Ask Mark what he thinks on the day in question, since his house overlooks the lakes and he can see how things are going. Catch and release means just that. When the fish is played out you net it gently, keeping it in the water, and slip out the hook. Turn the fish free of the net, and go looking for another one! Hooks must be barbless, or you must crush the barb using a pair of pliers. Should you have a smaller fish of up to 3 lb you can sometimes slide your hand down the leader and shake out the hook by gripping the shank firmly, not even bothering to net the fish at all. If you wish to keep your biggest trout, then by all means do so. I confess that I found it strange to be returning trout between 5 lb and 8 lb, but after you've been a few times you soon get used to it. (For 1989 Mark is introducing 'catch and retain' tickets. Prices on application.)

The opening hours of the fishery are from 8.30 AM until dark, and the scale of ticket charges for 1989 are as follows:

Day ticket: £15.00. The largest fish may now be kept. All others killed are chargeable at the rate of £1.45 per pound. This may change as market values fluctuate.
Half-day ticket: £12.00 (up to or from 2 PM). Evening ticket: £9.00 (from 4.30 PM). The average weight of each fish fluctuates, but can go as high as 5 lb.

The fishery record for a four-fish limit (killed) is 32 lb 12 oz. The rainbow record is 11 lb 2 oz and the brown record 6 lb 10 oz. The number of rods is also strictly limited to allow for freedom of movement from one lake to another, and with free tea and coffee on tap, you really can't go wrong. There is tackle for hire, flies for sale, parking and picnic area and a southern water rod licence is included in the ticket price.

Groups of eight anglers or more can get reduced rates. Located just outside the city of Salisbury, at West Grimstead, Walden's is a real eye-opener, and a day spent there is just the job if you have been struggling at other waters.

For more information, contact: Mark Dawson, Walden's Trout Fishery, Crockford Road, West Grimstead, Salisbury, Wiltshire. Telephone: (0722) 710480.

Back goes the author's 7 lb fish to provide sport for another day. Catch-and-release fisheries allow the angler to experiment more, thereby learning further methods of taking fish wary of the clumsy approach.

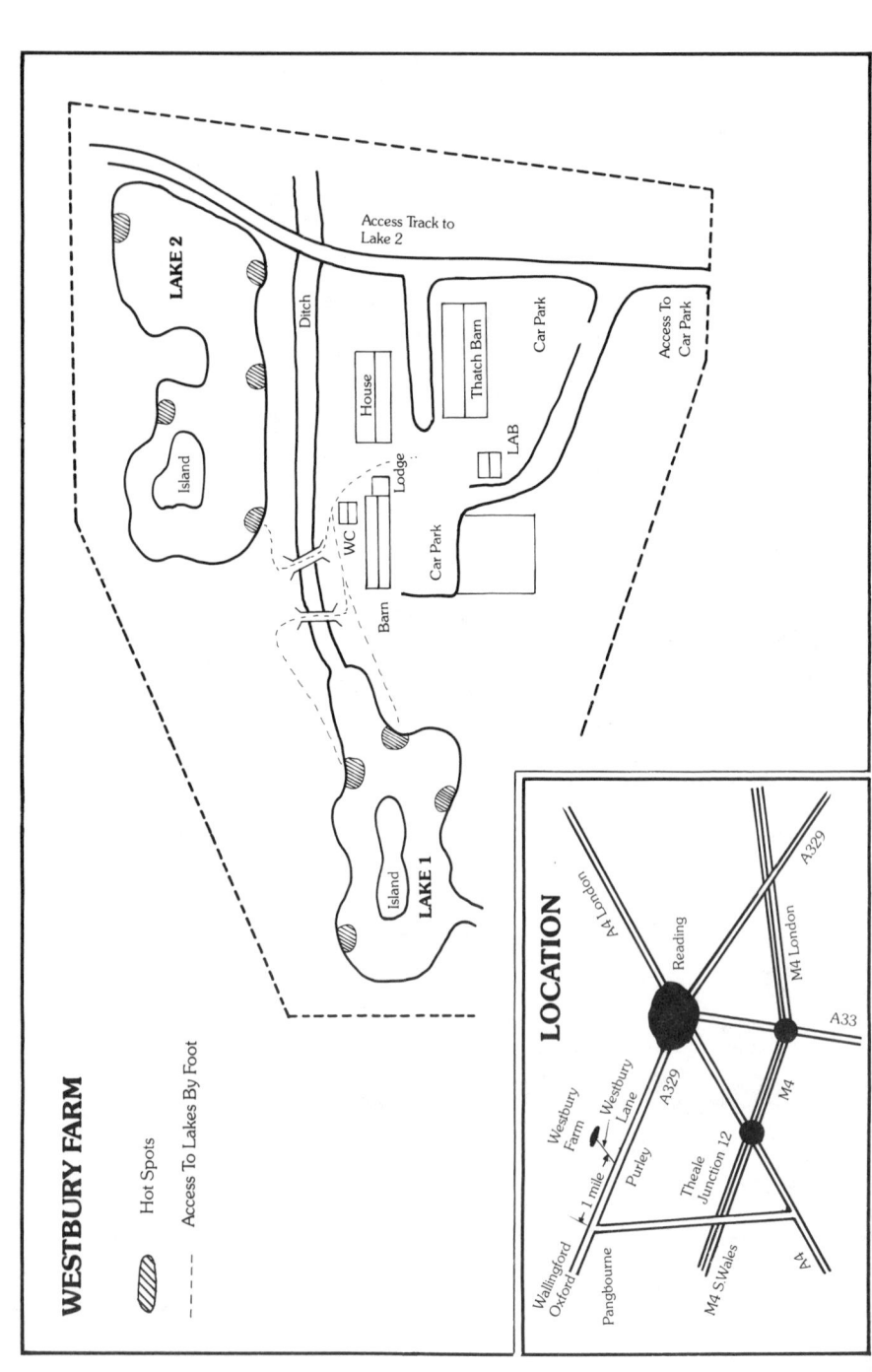

WESTBURY FARM

Hot Spots

Access To Lakes By Foot

LAKE 2

Access Track to Lake 2

Island

Ditch

House

Thatch Barn

Car Park

LAB

Access To Car Park

Lodge

WC

Car Park

Barn

Island

LAKE 1

LOCATION

A4 London

Reading

A329

M4 London

A33

A33

M4

Westbury Farm

Westbury Lane

1 mile

A329

Purley

Theale Junction 12

M4

Wallingford Oxford

Pangbourne

M4 S.Wales

A4

WESTBURY FARM

Although a few of the trout may be small in acreage, strict rod limitations mean you still get space to move around freely. One such venue is Westbury Farm, a small trout fishery nestling in the sheltered beauty of the Thames Valley. Nationally, it is probably still unknown to many, but it offers good sport in peaceful surroundings, which to most of us is what a good day's trout fishing is about. We all have that craving at some time or other to crash out as many fish as we can in the shortest possible time. It's a quite natural desire, but with catch-and-release waters like Walden's near Salisbury, you should be able to relieve some of those outlets, and thus enjoy the smaller put-and-take fisheries more.

Westbury Farm consists of just two lakes referred to, quite simply, as Lake One and Lake Two. The owner is Mr B. H. Theobald, who is as happy to have one person fishing as ten. His aim is for the fishermen to have some peace and solitude, with time to take in the surroundings of the valley. Lake One was excavated in 1976, during that long hot summer, and Lake Two was dug a year later. The total water area of the combined lakes is some seven acres, and they are in the middle of a 200-acre working farm, and with the pleasant backdrop of a vineyard. This is one of the first vineyards planted on the high-terrace system, and Mr Theobald is the only person to make red wine in this area in any sort of commercial quantity. This has nothing to do with the fishing, but I still feel it may be of interest to some of you who like to know a bit more about the background and management of a fishery.

I certainly learned a lot from Mr Theobald, who often gives tours of the vineyard and will lecture on the subject to those who wish to listen. The grapes from this vineyard are used for making rosé, red, and no fewer than ten different white wines, and there are 16 acres of planted vines. There is also a wine shop on the fishery so if you have had a reasonable day's sport you can treat yourself to something from the range of Westbury Wines. The vines themselves are over 15 years old, and careful management can lead to anything between 60,000 and 100,000 bottles a year being produced. With our inclement weather, production fluctuates, but it is gratifying to know not all good wines are imported.

The water on the two lakes can have a very slight tinge of colour, due, I suspect, to the typical black valley peat of the area. Depths fluctuate between 3 ft and 15 ft, giving the fly fisherman plenty of scope for a range of lines. The Thames valley is quite wide and winds can often funnel down it, but as a general rule it is fishable in most conditions. An east wind is the kiss of death for most forms of fishing, and painfully apparent in trout fishing. A warm, soft south-westerly that puts a light ripple on the water is deemed by regulars to be most productive, so give Mr Theobald a ring before you set off, to check how any breeze has affected the fishing.

APPROACH AND TACKLE

Line sizes need not be large as Westbury really comes into the category of a tiny fishery. Put away the forward-tapper No. 9s, roll up your shooting heads, and hang up the 10 ft carbon reservoir poles. Westbury Farm is what I class as a light tackle water. Stocked with quality rainbows of 2–5 lb, it really is a place for the brook rod enthusiast, who enjoys using No. 6 lines. Of course if you must get across to the other bank without walking, use a slow sinking Airflo in the deeper areas, searching out the bigger fish on a cold, blustery day.

I prefer the light floating line, leaded nymph, and slow retrieve across the surface, waiting for that sharp tweak of the line. You have to watch the end of the line for any signs of the fly being intercepted, and even then lift swiftly into a fish before it has time to eject your offering. It sounds easy, but converting those takes into fish on the bank takes a bit of getting used to. A day spent at the water in this way will certainly stand you in good stead on other fisheries.

The last time I fished Westbury, it was a cold day, yet Dave Sindle

This rainbow illustrates the high quality of fish stocked at Westbury Farm. As a general rule, the smaller buzzers and nymphs work best.

and Mick Honeybell from nearby Reading admitted how much they enjoyed their sport there, with both normally catching their limit of rainbows. There are no really thick weedbeds and no special fishery rules except a ban on the use of lures. Quite honestly, you only need a small fly anyway, and I would be suprised if you couldn't get a take all day on most of the popular nymphs in use.

The water has a high pH value and therefore the fish maintain a good body weight over a reasonable period there. As it is a small venue, try to give other anglers a bit of room and don't crowd them out even if they *are* catching fish. Most likely you will eventually end up on speaking terms and it may be to your advantage to see what the fish are coming out on.

SEASONAL TACTICS

Spring

No lures are allowed, but plenty of fish will come out anyway, on a variety of large nymphs. I see no reason to list any specials, as this early on almost anything will be catching. Colour is more important, and I would suggest starting with large nymphs of the following colours: white, black, and orange. If you can't get a fish on a nymph with one of those colours in it, especially at the start of the season, throw your tackle in the water and take up golf. As for lines, I still prefer a slow sink despite the fact that some of the 'experts' advise floaters. A slow sink allows you to fish a nymph on a horizontal plane, whereas a floating line will make your nymph rise and fall as you retrieve. Leader tippets of around 5 lb should be fine, because there is always the risk of hitting an overwintered fish early on.

Summer

To my mind, summer is the best time to tackle this tiny fishery. May can either be termed late spring or early summer. I always diary it as early summer because it is the first month you can really fish a dry fly with any degree of confidence. The mayfly season is very long for some reason best known to the mayfly. At Westbury it may go on for up to six weeks and last well into June. Perhaps there is something in that peaty soil as a mineral content that suits the reproductive style of the mayfly. You also have the hawthorn fly to imitate. The pattern I find most successful is the Black Aggravator, originally designed for slow-retrieve sinking lines. Then you have a really unusual insect, which you are unlikely to find on any other fishery. It is the grape black fly, most abundant when the flowers on the vines at the back of the lakes are in blossom. I doubt whether you can find a true match in your fly wallet, so use the nearest you can, and check with Mr Theobald first as to size and colour. For lines use only No. 6 floaters for dry fly and surface film nymphing, working around any area that the breeze is blowing into. Trout soon recognize where the food is going, and the slightest surface air drift, even without causing a ripple, will catch the insects' transparent wings and drift them into a corner. Remember to search out the bank edges with a nymph as well. I can't tell you how many anglers miss out on fish that are only a few yards away from them – not straight out, but right or left!

The larger lake offers good surface sport, even early in the season. Here an angler slides the net under a Westbury rainbow.

Autumn

This is the time of year to use the big nymphs, and this is possible on a slow-sinking line with a lightly greased leader. That way you can bump the fly along the bottom and pick up the bigger autumn rainbows. Slow retrieves should produce best. By contrast, for the floating line enthusiast there will still be cruising fish to be taken, but it will be on small black pennells and buzzers, with the leader strength dropped down to 3 lb. Again slow, steady retrieves will work best, and play any trout a bit gingerly until you have gauged his size. Autumn can be the time when the larger trout show up when you least expect them, and fishing being what it is, you end up with the biggest trout taking the smallest fly and lightest leader.

GENERAL INFORMATION

Fishing times are from 9 AM until half an hour after sunset, and other members of the family are allowed on the fishery provided they are under strict control. There is a car park and a WC on the fishery, which is located at Purley, near Reading, in Berkshire. The fishery is open from 1 April to 31 October and prices for 1989 are as follows:

Full rod: £300.00
Half rod: £160.00
A day ticket (four-fish limit) costs £16.50. Half-day ticket £9.50.
I would advise booking in advance as this quiet water has a strict rod limit.

For more information contact: B. H. Theobald, Westbury Trout Farm, Purley, Nr Reading, Berkshire. Telephone: Pangbourne (07357) 3123.

Four plump rainbows, and they all fought every inch of the way to the frying pan! Westbury Farm is a quiet fishery, offering seclusion and good fishing without the crowds of the big reservoirs.

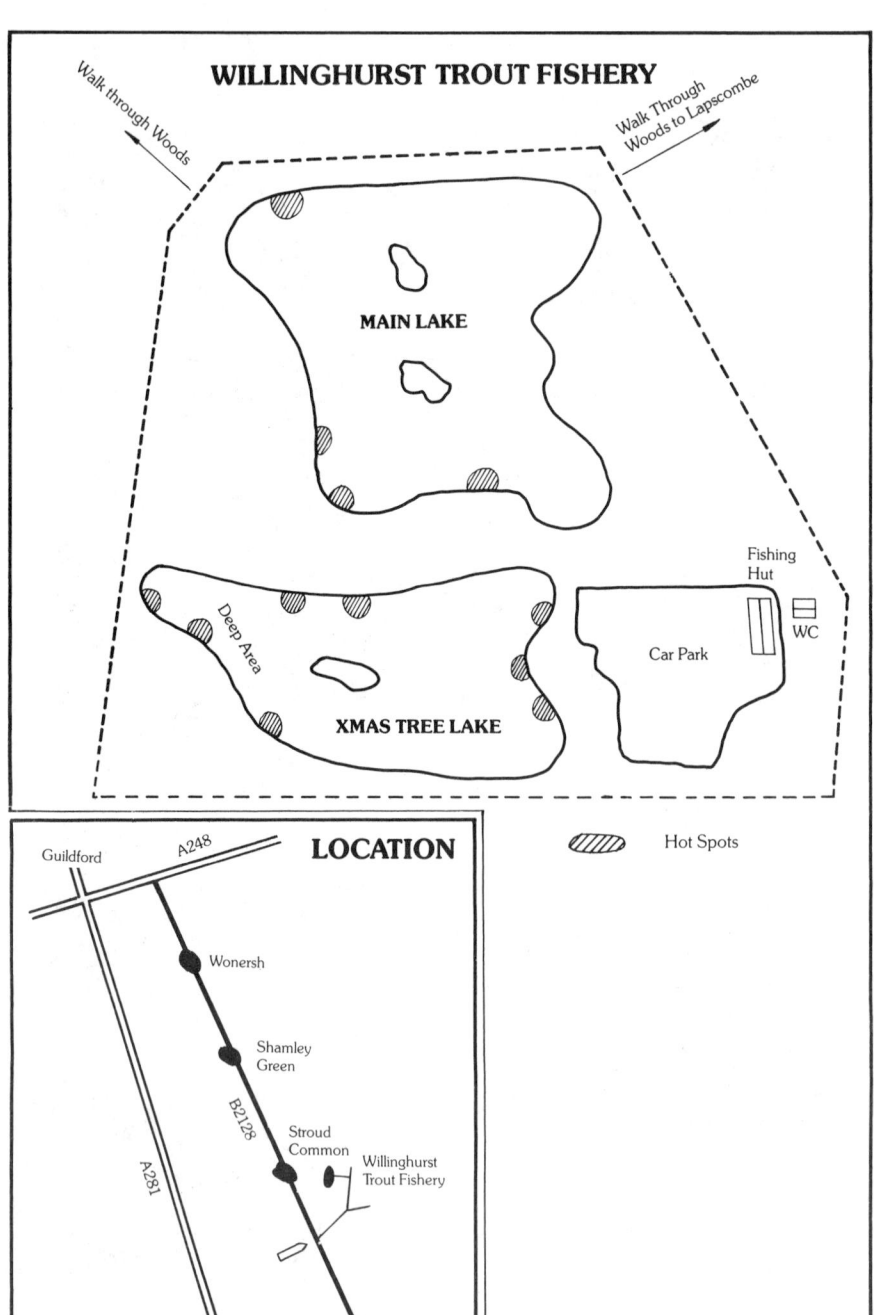

WILLINGHURST TROUT FISHERY

Walk through Woods

Walk Through Woods to Lapscombe

MAIN LAKE

Deep Area

XMAS TREE LAKE

Fishing Hut

Car Park

WC

Hot Spots

LOCATION

Guildford

A248

Wonersh

Shamley Green

B2128

A281

Stroud Common

Willinghurst Trout Fishery

Cranleigh

WILLINGHURST

As this venue is fairly local to me I have watched it grow into the considerable acreage of productive trout water it is today. Tucked away near Guildford in Surrey, it is in the vicinity of Shamley Green, one of the best kept areas of typical English countryside. Willinghurst is a water that you can visit at any time of the year, at any time of the day, and still be in with the chance of taking a fish or two.

The quality of the rainbows stocked is high indeed, and, incidentally, I am pleased to see most fishery owners now demanding a high standard of fish for their clients. The popularity of this water has grown not only because it keeps giving the angler good fishing, but because the fishery owner, Mark Syms, keeps the surrounding land as natural as possible. It is very easy to unwind here without that need to rush out onto the water and crack out your limit quickly before the next angler does.

Much of Willinghurst's all-day productivity comes not just from a high stocking policy, but because the water has a slight tinge of colour in it. In clear-water venues you can usually spot a fish, then stalk it round the fishery, making several casts in front of it and so giving it ample opportunity to see the fly. Owing to this slight colour, the main lakes at Willinghurst tell you nothing about the direction a trout takes when he has refused your fly the first time. I would guess that after an abortive take or follow the average angler would cast straight back out to the same place and commence his retrieve.

In clear water you would find the trout turns either one way or the other, and would then make your next cast accordingly. So why not do the same in coloured water, and make that next cast to one side or the other? Obviously there is a 50 per cent chance that your fly will cover the fish next time. Small things like this make for interesting small water trout fishing.

I well remember one year reporting that this water had a fish-per-rod average of 2.9, and that was way back in 1980, so it is good to see that Mark has maintained the stocking density. Given the natural scenery of the surrounding Surrey hills, it is easy to see how the idea of forming a trout fishery here came about. The main lake, situated near the car park was first excavated in early 1970s, the spoils from the construction being used for the dam, where deep water is in front of you. A glance at the sloping degree of the dam wall behind you gives you a fair indication of the depths in front. Here it drops away to some 12 ft, although any small lure fished about 2 ft below the surface seems to catch well. I find it strange that in many deeper, slightly coloured small venues that the trout aren't always grubbing about on the bottom. I know at times they do of course, because I have fished a fast-sink line and greased leader, dragging a stick fly back over the bottom.

There are a couple of islands in the centre of the main lake, with depths of 10 ft and 12 ft on your right hand bank and 8–10 ft on your left. Opposite the dam wall the water level shallows somewhat to about 6 ft and this area is productive later in the season when the rainbows harass the fry in towards the bank. There are three other tiny lakes, not much bigger than ponds really, but they are worth visiting, if only for a walk through the woods. I have never seen so many bluebells: on your first visit of the spring it is like walking through a carpeted fairyland to a miniature lake full of trout.

Two of these lakes, called Ash and Alder, are deceptive to the untrained eye. Yes, they seem very small, but I have had some really interesting fishing there, using a tiny brook rod and a slow-sink line. Neither lake fishes well if there are a few anglers working it at the same time. Far better if you can have it to yourself and let the occupants settle down a bit. Even ten minutes after other anglers have left you can sometimes see the odd rise or two as the trout regain confidence. Leave it a bit longer before fishing. There are a few carp in here as well, so if you see a few shapes drifting under the surface that fail to respond to your carefully presented fly, do not despair for they may well be carp!

There is also a third small lake worth trying. This one is called Lapscombe, and is a five-minute walk up the hill through the opposite wood and level with a gravel road. One end is overgrown, but as it is on a higher level than the other lakes, the water should be a lot cleaner. You may see the odd trout, but it is dark, deep water, so make sure you actually see your fly before you lift off for the back cast. And watch that cast as well. I have left many flies up those trees and bushes when I have been just a little too enthusiastic to cover that 'out-of-reach' rise. This is a water that fishes best on an overcast day, but keep your leader strengths down because of the clarity of the water. Use the same brook rod or generally lighter tackle as suited to Ash and Alder.

In the last few years Mark has added two more lakes to make this an extensive and versatile fishery. One was excavated near the car park and called Christmas Tree lake because it backs onto some of Mark's Christmas tree plantation. It is nearly as large as the main lake, with a small island in the centre, and inherits that very slight tinge of colour. You couldn't call it peat- or mud-coloured, more of a milky green, but it ensures that trout can be taken throughout the day. Although a recently formed lake it seemed to drop right into line with the others and the fish are in spanking condition. Depths range from 5–6 ft near the car park, to 10 ft along either side, and right down to 18 ft at the opposite end.

Finally there is Bluebell lake, situated along one of the wooded lanes. It was originally an irrigation lake for the Christmas tree plantation and then Mark put a small stock of carp in there, keeping it closed for fishing. Now several years later the carp have thrived to such an extent that you can occasionally take them on a fly. The plan for this lake at the moment is to open it as a 60-peg coarse fishery, but to incorporate it into the trout fishery during the close season. Again only a small water to fish, but with a stock of trout in it that still have to be caught.

The lake is U-shaped, with depths of 10–12 ft at one end and 4–8 ft at the other. Much of the surrounding land has a base of green-sand over clay, and presumably it is this that gives the two main lakes their milky appearance. With sand and clay mixed, there are a lot of springs which are affected by seasonal changes of rainfall.

The four smaller lakes, being shallower and clearer, all have a bit of weed in them, but quite distinctive surface weed, rather than silkweed

Christmas Tree Lake at Willinghurst is one of the most recently dug at this fishery, and produces the goods too, as this haul of rainbows shows. A variety of small lures and nymphs work well here.

on the bottom. The larger two lakes have little or no weed, which, I presume, is because the sunlight struggles to get through to the lake beds. The year of 1987, as at so many of the other waters in this guide, was Willinghurst's best-ever season. The two main and four small lakes took a total of 10,362 trout. Of these, 725 were over 4 lb and the top fish was a rainbow weighing in at 10 lb 4 oz. The fishery records are 12 lb for rainbow trout and 8 lb 4 oz for brown.

APPROACH AND TACKLE

While almost any fly or lure will take fish at some time or other, the following come as a recommendation from Mark and are worth trying at some stage of the day or season: Montana nymph, Damsel Fly, Pheasant Tail, Viva, Appetiser, Jack Frost and small lead-headed flies. For the dry-fly enthusiast there is a major hatch of mayfly between 15 May and 15 June. They can litter the surface like great dark butterflies. Very often it is worth waiting until evening to get the best fun on this artificial fly. Finally, the good old Daddy Longlegs also brings fish. Generally speaking, the sedges give you enough surface activity during the early part of the season, particularly if we have a warm spring.

As for the size of tackle to use, the versatility of this venue means it is definitely worth packing a couple of outfits. For the main lake I would advise the standard 9–9½ ft rod, rated 6/7 and loaded with a weight-forward corresponding line. Keep your leader lengths long, at least 10 ft, stretching to 15 ft during the dog-days of midsummer. Then for the tiny lakes or ponds, a regular glass or carbon brook rod will enable you to poke around in those difficult-to-reach corners, and give you some fine sport should you hook a two-pounder or larger. A rod length of 6½–7 ft and a reel loaded with No. 5/6 double-taper line will be fine.

Although I have classified Willinghurst as a small water, I think it is worth taking a big reservoir rod, around 9½ ft long, coupled to a weight-forward No. 8 floating line. There are islands in both of the larger lakes, and you just *know* the trout patrol around the edges, especially on a windy day. Don't forget insects and other food drift

Take advantage of any ripple at Willinghurst to fish a surface fly round towards the windward bank. Here an angler hits into a fish that followed his fly for several yards before taking.

onto the windward side of these islands, for the floating line enables you to fish slowly, almost along the edges. It's a long throw, but with a small lure, on a windy day, you can pick up not only the bonus fish, but some of the larger fish as well.

SEASONAL TACTICS

Spring

Start off with a slow-sink Airflo line, and stick to the smaller lures tied after Appetiser, Viva, and similar patterns. Fish quite quickly with your retrieve so you can cover more ground, moving around the larger of the two lakes and covering the deeper ends first. Try the small lakes later, for April will bring plenty of action with the sedges on Ash and Alder. Springtime will see the wooded floor smothered with bluebells, one of the beautiful sights so rare in the English countryside now. Always check first with Mark to see what his advice is on fishing the small lakes.

Summer

Hard fishing and easy fishing. The easier part will be from mid-May to mid-June when the two larger lakes have their prolific hatch of mayfly. You can fish the Mayfly nymph during the daytime, and then go onto dry Mayfly from about 5 PM. Stay on until dusk as this final hour can see the water come alive. In July and early August any trout water gets harder. Then is the time to fish a floating line, a 15 ft leader, and a tiny buzzer or lightly leaded nymph. There is no need for a fast retrieve – just inch it across the surface, watching the end of the line for signs of a take. Don't expect a rod-wrenching pull – all you will get is a tweak, so it is up to you to set that hook with a flick of the wrist. The bigger rainbows of 3 lb and upwards will fall for this, even at midday, although early morning and last light are better.

Autumn

There should be some fry feeders about, cruising the margins as they harass their prey. Make your casts using either floating line or a slow sink, along the edge of the bank, only some 3 ft out from the edge. Any lure pattern should catch and don't forget to try as well some of those larger nymph patterns, which are very nearly the same size as many lures. September can be good for the Daddy Longlegs off the surface, mainly from the larger two lakes. Remember to try the reservoir rod and heavier line to reach the fringes of those islands.

Guildford angler Adrian Hutchins landed this quart of trout using a slow-sink line and a Mayfly nymph. Late May and early June can see a lot of surface activity with this insect. Other good patterns in summer are Damsel, Green Beast, and Hawthorn fly.

Winter

As Willinghurst is a year-round venue, it will be in your own interest to phone Mark first if the weather looks at all clear and still. Nothing is worse than arriving at the water after a long drive to find a sheet of ice across it. For those who make the best of our winter months, the use of the lead-headed flies with Marabou tails come into their own. The smaller models work best, and I personally favour just three colours: white, black and orange, and fish them in that order. The best movement in the water on these 'flies' comes when they are coupled to the floating line, the weight near the hook eye making them sink very quickly. A sinking line will see you dragging leaves and twigs from the lake bed, so try and persevere with the floating line. In winter you should spend only a short time on the small ponds in the woods. Just give them a brief going over, although stay on longer if you take a fish, and then go back to the large lakes.

GENERAL INFORMATION

Willinghurst is open 365 days a year, with an opening time of 9 AM and closing time at dusk. A toilet, a fishing hut with scales, and a picnic area complete the picture. This is the ideal place to scrounge a day away from the family. You can fish while they go touring Guildford before returning to share lunch with you at one of the picnic tables.

Finally, Mark will give instruction to beginners and only charge them when they catch a fish. The quality of both surroundings and fishing at Willinghurst gives excellent value for money and the venue is well worth more than one visit.

The cost breakdown for standard limit bags is as follows:

Day permit: £16.50.

Half-day permit: £13.50.

Evening permit: £9.50.

A full-day season permit costs £140.00.

For more information contact: Mark Syms, Willinghurst Trout Fishery, Willinghurst, Shamley Green, Surrey GU5 0SU. Telephone: Guildford (0483) 275048.

OTHER SMALL WATERS

While I have been able to give extensive details on many of the leading trout fisheries in Southern England, there are still literally dozens that cannot be included for reasons of space. Perhaps I shall save detailed analysis of more waters of interest to the travelling fly fisherman until another guide book. Nevertheless, I feel it is worth listing some of them, so that you can at least experiment with other places.

Small water trout fishing is, in my opinion, fairly standardized. Because they are small, there is no way that such waters can hold enough insect and food life to sustain a large head of trout for anglers to catch daily. Therefore they must be restocked with fish on a weekly, twice-weekly, or daily basis. This is the only way that they can provide fishermen with a large enough head of big fish to keep them satisfied. Bearing this in mind, much of what I have said in this book can be applied to all other small waters.

If you wish to sample the delights of large open-water reservoirs, then a whole different rule applies. You need longer rods, heavier lines, different flies, and certainly different techniques. These are verging on true 'wild' trout waters, whereas the smaller fisheries are supplying a demand for instant fish. I find that whichever small water I visit, the same tactics, tackle, and even flies can be used over and over again. For this reason alone you should have no qualms at all about trying unfamiliar small waters for trout.

In Berkshire you have Pondwood Fishery at Maidenhead. Dave Gaskin runs this 1½-acre venue with a 10-angler limit, charging £21.00 for a day ticket with a five-fish limit on a full-day ticket.

Half-day and evening tickets are also available. Telephone (0734) 345527. In Buckinghamshire you will find at Mursley the famous Church Hill Farm. There are two lakes of 7½ and 2½ acres, with a fishing season from 17 March to 30 November. Day tickets give a four-fish limit and evening tickets two fish. Telephone (02967) 524. Latimer Park lakes near Chesham, again in Buckinghamshire, are 12 acres, with a stretch of the river Chess also available. They are stocked daily with rainbows and browns and the season runs from 2 April to 30 September. Boats are available on request. Fishing times are from 9 AM to dark. Telephone (02404) 2396. Near Milton Keynes is Vicarage Spinney Trout Fishery. Here there are six acres stocked with browns and rainbows. The fishery is open from 28 March to 28 February. Fishing is from 9 AM to dusk. A day ticket gives you four fish. After 2 PM a two-fish limit applies. Boats, single or double, are bookable. Book fishing in advance on (0908) 614969.

Down in Dorset you will find Flowers Farm Trout lakes. These total 3½ acres and are stocked with rainbows and brown trout. There is a single-fly rule and the maximum hook size is size 10. A full-day ticket gives a four-fish limit, a half-day ticket three fish, and an evening ticket two fish. The season starts on 1 March and advance booking is required. Telephone Cerne Abbas 351. Hermitage Lakes are also at Cerne Abbas, near Dorchester, with 2 acres stocked with both browns and rainbows. This one is open all year round for rainbows, and 24 March to 15 October for the browns. Telephone Holnest 556. Still in Dorset, there are 10 acres stocked with rainbow at Dorset Springs Trout lakes. A full-day ticket here gives you a five-fish limit, a half-day ticket four fish, and an evening ticket three fish. Telephone Sturminster Marshall 857653.

In Essex there is the big fish water of Aveley Lakes: 5 acres stocked with brooks, browns, and rainbows with a minimum size of 4 lb. Fishing is from 8 AM to dusk, and a full-day ticket gives you four fish, a half-day ticket two fish, and an evening ticket one fish. Boats are obtainable at fixed moorings. Telephone Purfleet (0708) 868425.

Back in Hampshire you have Chiphall lake near Bishop's Waltham. There is a traditional season start here of 1 April, with dry fly and nymph only. Telephone Bishop's Waltham 4845. Near Fordingbridge lies the famous Damerham. This was in its time probably the most famous day-ticket trout water, with a reputation for quality as well as large fish in beautiful surroundings. Certainly it must have been here that the first of the small-water visual stalking of individual fish came into being. There are six lakes stocked with both browns and rainbows, and fishing starts at 9.30 AM. Advance booking is required. Telephone (07253) 446.

Robinswood Fishery at Churt offers five acres stocked with both browns and rainbows. It is an all-year season starting from 1 April, and fishing times are 9 AM to dusk. A full-day ticket gives you a five-fish limit, and single fly only is the rule. Telephone (025125) 4321. In Hertfordshire is the larger Croxley Hall Waters. Here there are four lakes totalling 20 acres and they are stocked on a daily basis with both rainbows and browns. The season runs from 1 April to 31 October, a full-day ticket giving you a four-fish limit and an evening ticket a two-fish limit. Boats are available but no spectators are allowed. Telephone (0923) 778290. Tenterden Trout Lakes, in Kent, total five acres, with fishing times of 9 AM to one hour after sunset. Traditional flies only are allowed. Back down in Somerset, about eight miles south of Taunton are Otterhead Lakes. These are two 2½-acre lakes run by the Fisheries and Recreation Department. They open on 26 March. Fishing times are from 8 AM to one hour after sunset. There is a six-fish limit. Telephone (0278) 57333.

Powdermills fishery at Chilworth, near Guildford, offers a 3½ acre lake, a stream and a pond. Both brown and rainbow trout are stocked and fishing is from 8.30 AM until dusk. A full-day ticket gives you a four-fish limit, an afternoon or evening ticket a two-fish limit, and a half-day ticket gives you three fish.

In Sussex, the Wattlehurst Trout lake four miles north of Horsham on the A24 gives two acres of fishable water. It is a year-round venue stocked with rainbows and browns, and fishing is with fly only from 8 AM to 9.30 PM. Telephone 030 679341. Also in Sussex is Lakedown, at Burwash Common. The four lakes totalling some 16 acres offer excellent rainbow fishing with a variety of method restrictions. The season opens on 5 March, but shooting head lines are not allowed. Telephone Burwash 883449. Yew Tree Trout Fishery is at Rotherfield near Crowborough in Sussex and offers six acres stocked with rainbows. It is open all year and from 8 AM until one hour after dusk. A full-day ticket allows a four-fish limit, a morning ticket two fish, an afternoon ticket three fish, and an evening ticket two fish. Professional fly tuition is available, the maximum hook size is 10, and some boats are bookable on a day, half-day, and evening basis. Telephone Rotherfield 2529.

Finally, in Wiltshire you have Zeals Trout Fishery, two acres stocked with rainbows. The fishery open on 1 March and fishing times are 9 AM to sunset. A full-day ticket gives you four fish, and a half-day ticket two fish. There is a fly-only rule, lures being forbidden. Telephone (0747) 840573.

The above is just a quick list of other venues worth a trip. There are many more, but these recommendations, coupled with the detailed analysis of the main waters described, will give you enough trout fishing for at least a season. Remember that each venue is going to have a bad day at some time, so why not book a couple of days at each spacing your bookings by a month or so? In this way you will allow for any unusual weather or fishery conditions.

Nowadays, many small stillwaters cater to the increasing demand of the modern fly fisherman, but although we obviously have more trout fishermen than waters, you are still more likely to take your biggest-ever fly-caught trout on a small water. Much more likely, in fact, than on a reservoir, where the average size of trout is smaller, although the abundant space ensures that they are super-fit and harder scrappers. Good trouting!